Sport Governance Insights

This book introduces the fundamentals of sport governance, assuming no prior knowledge on the part of the reader. It explains to students and practitioners alike why governance matters and how it can be better practiced in sport organizations.

Introducing key concepts and the micro-processes of implementation, the book explains what governance is and why it has become increasingly important. It explains what sport boards do, and how they should function for sport organizations to be effective, and it provides practical tools to help ensure good governance.

Full of insights from cutting-edge research and real-world cases, this is essential reading for any student or practicing sport manager, administrator, or policy-maker who needs a concise introduction to this important topic.

Christos Anagnostopoulos is an Assistant Professor in sport management within the College of Science and Engineering at Hamad Bin Khalifa University (HBKU), Qatar. He is an editorial board member in nine international scientific journals related to sport management. He established the *UNESCO Chair on Governance and Social Responsibility in Sport* at UCLan Cyprus; he serves as the Director and one of the two co-chair holders.

Dimitra Papadimitriou is an Associate Professor and Vice Chair in the Department of Business Management at the University of Patras, Greece. Part of her research interest lies in organizational governance issues related to the organizational structure and board effectiveness of national sport federations. She teaches the sport organizational governance course, serving also as course coordinator, at the Sport Management Master Program of the Open Hellenic University, Greece.

Terri Byers is a Professor in the Faculty of Kinesiology at the University of New Brunswick, Canada. She has served on multiple sport club boards in equestrian sport and worked with the Sport Governance Academy in England on good governance tools and resources for all Tier 2 and 3 funded sport organizations. She has consulted for local and provincial sport organizations in New Brunswick, Canada, on improving strategic planning, managing conflict of interest and good governance. Current research projects focus on understanding barriers to increasing diversity in sport governance.

Grzegorz Botwina is an Assistant Professor in the Faculty of Management at the University of Warsaw, Poland, where he serves as Director of the Polish Olympic Research and Studies Centre. He is the elected President of the Polish Cycling Federation and CEO of the Institute for Sport Governance, an independent think tank focused on improving governance in sport organizations. He also created the Academy of Sport Management, a government-funded program for the national sport federations in Poland.

Sport Business Insights
Series Editors
Aaron C.T. Smith, *Loughborough University, UK*
Constantino Stavros, *RMIT University, Australia*

Sport Business Insights is a series that aims to cut through the clutter, providing concise and relevant introductions to an array of contemporary topics related to the business of sport. Readers – including passionate practitioners, curious consumers and sport students alike – will discover direct and succinct volumes, carefully curated to present a useful blend of practice and theory. In a highly readable format, and prepared by leading experts, this series shines a spotlight on subjects of currency in sport business, offering a systematic guide to critical concepts and their practical application.
    Available in this series:

Sport Branding Insights
Constantino Stavros and Aaron C.T. Smith

Sport Sponsorship Insights
Norm O'Reilly, Gashaw Abeza and Mark Harrison

Esports Insights
Emily Hayday, Holly Collison-Randall and Sarah Kelly

Stadia Naming Rights in Sport
Leah Gillooly, Terry Eddy and Dominic Medway

Sport Governance Insights
Christos Anagnostopoulos, Dimitra Papadimitriou, Terri Byers and Grzegorz Botwina

For more information about this series, please visit: https://www.routledge.com/Sport-Business-Insights/book-series/SBI

Sport Governance Insights

Christos Anagnostopoulos,
Dimitra Papadimitriou, Terri Byers,
and Grzegorz Botwina

LONDON AND NEW YORK

First published 2023
by Routledge
4 Park Square, Milton Park, Abingdon, Oxon OX14 4RN

and by Routledge
605 Third Avenue, New York, NY 10158

*Routledge is an imprint of the Taylor & Francis Group, an
informa business*

British Library Cataloguing-in-Publication Data
A catalogue record for this book is available from the British
Library

Library of Congress Cataloging-in-Publication Data
Names: Anagnostopoulos, Christos, 1978- author. |
Papadimitriou, Dimitra, author. | Byers, Terri, author. |
Botwina, Grzegorz, author.
Title: Sport governance insights / Christos Anagnostopoulos,
Dimitra Papadimitriou, Terri Byers and Grzegorz Botwina.
Description: Abingdon, Oxon ; New York, NY : Routledge,
2023. | Series: Sport business insights | Includes
bibliographical references and index.
Identifiers: LCCN 2022035815 | ISBN 9781032183954
(hardback) | ISBN 9781032183961 (paperback) | ISBN
9781003254324 (ebook)
Subjects: LCSH: Sports administration.
Classification: LCC GV713 .A53 2023 | DDC 796.06/9--dc23/
eng/20220810
LC record available at https://lccn.loc.gov/2022035815

ISBN: 978-1-032-18395-4 (hbk)
ISBN: 978-1-032-18396-1 (pbk)
ISBN: 978-1-003-25432-4 (ebk)

DOI: 10.4324/9781003254324

Typeset in Times
by KnowledgeWorks Global Ltd.

Contents

Foreword

It is a great privilege to have been asked to share my perceptions regarding this long overdue publication – Sport Governance Insights. In practice, few topics are more difficult to navigate, challenging, or multifaceted than governance reform. This is particularly true in the highly nuanced, diverse, and complex sport ecosystem. Moreover, there is always the elephant in the room that theory and practice are uneasy bedfellows when it comes to sports governance reform. However, just because something is difficult to achieve, this does not mean it cannot be explored, explained, and articulated in straightforward ways that are theoretically underpinned and yet lead to implementable action. This, in my opinion, is the absolute key to progressive and positive governance reform.

Sport Governance is receiving ever-increasing scrutiny from every corner of the stakeholder landscape. It is becoming clear to all that insufficient governance structures, a lack of organizational hygiene, low levels of transparency and integrity, and the notion of "marking your own homework" in terms of governance capacities and capabilities are not only unsustainable, but also detrimental to sport as an industry. This awareness and appetite for change is intrinsically linked to, and underpinned by, a growing awareness and intolerance of the consequences of low levels of governance that do not proactively address corruption, diversity and inclusion, health and safety, safeguarding, and every other aspect of sport. There can be no ambiguity we are experiencing a paradigm shift in sports governance and we are witnessing the consequences of both good and bad governance models play out in tangible ways across the board – including in bottom line, measurable ways such as public support, confidence, investment, and sponsorship.

The Sport Integrity Global Alliance (SIGA) is a global, independent, neutral coalition led by the sports industry and supported by key stakeholders. As such we promote best practices, a set of independently verified Universal Standards (including on Good Governance), and credible solutions to usher a new era of governance and integrity in sport. As the Senior Director of Research, Knowledge and Innovation at SIGA, I consider knowledge exchange a critical component of the successful delivery of our reform agenda and the implementation of Good Governance in Sport more broadly – at every level. As such, essential texts that succinctly articulate the core components of Good Governance in Sport and provide practical, actionable knowledge are instrumental to positive evolution. For these reasons, I am extremely pleased to say that this publication is one such text and thoroughly recommend it to all those currently working in sports governance and those aspiring to do so.

Dr. Iain Lindsay
Senior Director of Research, Knowledge and Innovation
The Sport Integrity Global Alliance (SIGA)
London, 3 June 2022

1 Introduction

On Your Mark, Get Set, Go!

Introduction

Welcome to *Sport Governance Insights*, part of the *Routledge Sport Business Insights* series, which offers concise and accessible introductions to various contemporary aspects of sport business. Sport governance has emerged as one of the most important contemporary aspects of sport organizations and an increasingly complex element of sport management. This is partly due to the increasingly complex environment of sport organizations and the growing commercialization and professionalization of sport. It is also because of the many examples of failures in sport governance that have been raised in the media, suggesting a need for research, education, and training on what sport governance is and should be and how to do it. This book provides clarity to industry professionals and students who may be new to sport governance.

More broadly, this book is one of the first outcomes of the recently established UNESCO Chair in Governance and Social Responsibility in Sport, at the University of Central Lancashire in Cyprus. All four authors of this book have a role in this UNESCO Chair. Christos Anagnostopoulos is the founder, co-chair holder, and the director. Dimitra Papadimitriou sits on the Scientific Committee and serves as one of the two coordinators of the Education & Training pillar. Terri Byers also sits on the Scientific Committee and serves as one of the two coordinators of the Research pillar. Greg Botwina, who is also on the Scientific Committee, is co-coordinator of the Dissemination & Outreach pillar.

The chair's activities are in line with UNESCO's priorities on Education and Social and Human Sciences (and the intersection thereof). More specifically, the focus is on providing national and international leadership in education with a view to addressing poor

DOI: 10.4324/9781003254324-1

governance mechanisms and irresponsible activities in the sport sector. Acknowledging that UNESCO seeks to promote the development and the practice of sporting activities to foster social integration in different cultural and political contexts, the chair underscores that the governance of sport institutions that have assumed such a responsibility has a bearing on the quality and impact of the designed sport programs and interventions, and consequently on the (end-) users/beneficiaries. Thus, in the context of this UNESCO Chair, which corresponds to a formal education system, activities will be developed through appropriate partnerships in order to ensure that good governance principles (such as equity, effectiveness, accountability, rule of law, participation, and democracy) are understood and appreciated so that they can be effectively applied to/by institutions that use sport as an enabler for sustainable development.

Focus: Why a Book on Sport Governance?

Sport governance is an aspect of sport organizations that has received increasing attention from scholars and practitioners. While sport governance was primarily a concern for national and international larger sport organizations, it is now a topic of concern for even small voluntary sport clubs, to improve the operation and inclusion of sport organizations at all levels across the globe. The term "good governance" has become a prominent term and goal across the Western world of sport, but what constitutes good, or effective governance may be defined differently in different cultures. However, this book does not intend to get into the debate around cultural interpretations of sport governance. Rather, we aim to provide a practical guide for sport organizations, and students who may be new to the practice of sport governance, to understand what this term means in practice, and how it can be used in sport organizations to improve the function and delivery of sport. In short, sport governance is something that can offer real value to sport organizations and should not be thought of or used as a "tick box" exercise of compliance to regulations and internal/external policy.

While the research and literature on sport governance is growing, with increasing attention to critical perspectives of governance practice in sport, this book offers something new to the knowledge base. True to the *Sport Business Insight* series, it cuts through the complexities of sport governance to provide an accessible introduction to thinking about and doing governance in sport organizations, with the aim of improving the management of sport and the impact sport has on society.

Structure of the Book

As the next chapter will show, sport governance is a complex process within sport organizations and can present challenges to sport development and management. However, it is important to first gain an understanding of fundamental components of governance and governance in sport. We do this and begin to introduce some of the more dynamic aspects of sport governance, so that people who are new to governance in sport or students wishing to gain some initial understanding can bring this knowledge directly to sport organizations. Each chapter title takes the form of a question in order to provide a clear focus for what readers will learn, with the answer to that question provided throughout the chapter but also summarized in the conclusion of each chapter. Excluding the introductory one, the book has seven more chapters (questions) that focus on fundamental issues in sport governance such as board behavior, structure and processes, board composition, and strategy.

Sport Governance Insights provides the fundamental knowledge needed to define sport governance and to realize the importance of good governance in sport. The book also highlights some complexities of working in sport governance, whether as a volunteer board member or an executive, paid member of staff. Each chapter of this book focuses on an important aspect of sport governance, to help understanding of WHAT is governance? Yet this is not enough to know *"HOW can we achieve good governance in sport?"* To address the how, three themes permeate throughout the book that point to the skills/activities needed to achieve good governance in sport organizations: communication, diversity/inclusion, and change. These themes are interdependent and dynamic, which we illustrate below and throughout each chapter.

"Communication" is a key theme throughout this book and is a key concern in all aspects of society, business, sport, and human life. Without understanding how to communicate, how communication varies, and how to improve communication, it is not possible to coordinate or achieve group or organizational goals. With the increasing complexity of sport organizations and the sport ecosystem, the need for clear, coordinated, and open communication within the board, between the board members and executive(s), and with wider stakeholders is essential for providing good governance and high-quality sport management. Communication in this fashion contributes directly to transparency of organizational operations and decision-making, which helps sport organizations avoid the negative consequences of conflict of interests, corruption, and stakeholder

uncertainty. So, beyond the scope of this book, but essential to the education and training of governance professionals, is continuous learning of the many intricacies of communication and how these vary by culture, age, race, or other factors. This book highlights the importance of communication and offers some initial guidance on effective communication in structures, interpersonal relations, and group synergies, but further understanding is needed of how boards communicate, the role of bias in decision-making, the impact of diversity on performance, and how to manage increasing diversity and complexity in sport organizations.

The second theme running through the book is *"diversity/inclusion,"* which relates directly to communication and the broader notion of sport governance. There has been a growing trend in sport to be more inclusive of diverse populations, of participants in sport, of volunteers, and of those serving the boards. Increasing inclusion has proved challenging for sport organizations around the globe. Inclusion begins with increasing diversity but also requires ongoing attention to an environment that is welcoming, respectful, and inclusive of the new and different ideas that come with greater diversity. Being more inclusive of gender, sex, race, age, ethnicity, and/or disability increases the complexity of the organization and presents increased uncertainty to appropriate communication, so time is needed to adjust when new people or groups are added to existing structures and cultures of sport organizations. Taking communication and inclusion together, we can see many sport organizations and boards striving for more reflexive communication (the generative mode of governance: see Chapter 4), where stakeholders have a voice in decisions rather than top-down decision-making with little consultation or consideration of implications to stakeholders. While we cover conscious planning and decision-making to be more inclusive, there is still much to learn about the impact of unconscious biases or ableism in sport governance and inclusive intentions. Unconscious bias may be a more powerful inhibitor to responsible governance in sport than any other factors, as it is usually not recognized and can be difficult to discuss formally.

The third theme running throughout the book is *"change,"* recognizing that change is constant in all sport organizations, including that of sport governance structures and practices. While change results in varying degrees of uncertainty and may be perceived as negative, we like to think of and encourage you to think of change as a positive aspect of sport governance. Sport organizations and boards should recognize that not all changes need to happen at once. The focus of this book on different modes or layers of governance, including a strategic focus, and use of committees to enhance board function, means that sport governance will change over time and leaders should think about the pace and sequence of change needed in their organizations. This means that if your organization recognizes, through evaluation processes, that improvements in governance are needed, this is quite normal and expected. Planning for change, education of board members, new committees needed to inform complex problems, or increases in policies given challenges in the environment in which the sport operates, should all be seen as opportunities to increase effectiveness and move closer to providing high-quality and ethical care of sport stakeholders. When we consider this theme in conjunction with our thoughts on communication and inclusion, we really start to see how complex governance can be in the context of sport. At times, sport can be under tremendous pressure to improve, change, or even eradicate poor governance practices and many sport organizations are actively working toward improving their governance or working on total governance reform. In reality, however, most change in organizations is resisted, which can be due to divergent interests, lack of resources and/or knowledge, power incongruence, or more sinister problems in sport organizations from conflict of interest and corruption. There is much to learn about the "dark side" of sport governance if we are to understand how to manage resistance to change. While much research has focused on what is tangible and observable in sport governance, a larger challenge exists in terms of examining the intangible aspects of governance generally and change, diversity/inclusion, and communication more specifically.

Overall, this book takes a straightforward and practical approach to governance in sport and recognizes that the reality of sport governance is more complex than can be covered in one introductory book. However, our aim has been to provide a positive, yet slightly critical, overview of sport governance to enable those new (but not solely new...) to the field to gain some confidence regarding what is involved in sport governance, how to build or revise good governance practices, and to think to the future so that reflexive and responsible practices can be implemented in sport to ensure ethical and safe sport for all stakeholders.

Specifically, the book is structured as follows:

Chapter 2: What is sport governance? This chapter begins by providing examples of what sport governance is, avoiding philosophical debates and cutting to the essence of what it is and why we do it.

Chapter 3: How do boards in sport behave? This chapter offers readers some prominent theory to understand the practice of governance. Each theory provides a piece of the puzzle and some insight into board behavior. Depending on which perspective or lens we use, we can understand different aspects of governance.

Chapter 4: Inside the Sport Boardroom: What's the score? This chapter discusses the roles with interlinked responsibilities and tasks of the board members, but emphasizes the three governance modes that at play when governance is exercised: the fiduciary, the strategic, and – the least applied – generative mode, which calls for an unbiased, self-critical thinking of why boards do (or will/should do) what they do.

Chapter 5: Sport board composition: Who's making up the board? Here we demonstrate the need for skilled board members and how committees can help boards function more effectively, through accessing a wider variety of expertise and skill than found on the board. Because there is no such thing as a perfect board, committees serve an essential function to informing the decision-making process for boards. Here, we discuss not only strategic but also critical thinking and how this can benefit boards and governance.

Chapter 6: The strategic governance mode: What does it mean in practice for sport organizations? This chapter adds another layer to understanding sport governance by suggesting that governance should be strategic rather than reactionary. This further emphasizes that governance should not be thought of as a "tick box" exercise of compliance, but as a long-term tool to enhance the operation and performance of a sport organization.

Chapter 7: Effective sport boards: How can committees help? Here we highlight the point that boards are not static; they change, and the requirements and skills needed for effectiveness also change as new issues or challenges arise that the board must analyze and for which decisions are needed. Committees, overseen by the board, offer a valuable opportunity to enrich the board's ability to make informed and high-quality decisions and this chapter outlines how committees can contribute to greater sport governance effectiveness.

Chapter 8: CEO and sport boards: Who's the boss? The final chapter of this book reveals a key relationship to building good governance in sport organizations. While there is sometimes some confusion over the different roles and responsibilities between the board and the executive/CEO, we offer some thoughts on how to differentiate the roles and facilitate good synergies between the two. It is useful to think of the board and CEO as a relationship rather than hierarchy where there is only one "boss."

Thank you for choosing this book. While we acknowledge that sport governance is a complex topic, we have attempted to offer a starting point to understanding a developing yet important activity of sport organizations. We hope you enjoy this book and, most importantly, find it useful for practicing sport governance. We take a very practical approach, integrating some theory along the way, because the practice of sport governance has been in development longer than scholarship on sport governance. Also, sport governance presents challenges for sport managers, who often work or volunteer in sport organizations because of their interest or passion for sport, not governance. Yet, principles of good governance in sport have been developed across many industrialized countries, governments have mandated sport organizations demonstrate good governance to receive public funding, in several countries. This increasing use of governance in sport (or the codification thereof) has been fairly rapid, and scholarly activity to understand and evaluate impact of governance within and on sport organization performance and operations is understandably slower. Sport management and governance is different from governance seen in many other organizations, nonprofit or commercial companies. Sport organizations are prone to complexities that require governance, but resistance to the formalization that governance brings, due to the competing values and dedication between sport itself and the commercialization/professionalization of sport organizations. For example, sport organizations are very often run by a combination of volunteers (from Presidents and entire boards to teams of volunteers for events or day-to-day operations or coaches), and paid staff (from coaches to front office and CEOs). Volunteers, and even some paid professional staff, may have little interest or knowledge of "governance" but do have a passion for sport, for providing the best service to athletes, the best competition to teams, and/or the best pathway for athletes to achieve elite performance. Governance, therefore, can be seen as contrary to those goals as it takes time to learn what governance is and how to do it. However, as we will illustrate in this book, governance can be the tool to achieve multiple goals in sport and is not an activity in opposition to enjoying sport, but it is a mechanism to ensure safe and inclusive sport, quality, and inclusive decision-making as well as high quality, ethical, sport experiences for a wide range of participants.

Sport governance is also different from governance in other industries because context matters. We continue to identify unique elements of governance in sport throughout the book, such as Chapter 2, which highlights the role of athletes in representation in sport organizations, and increasingly the governance of sport. Athletes are the focus on the service provided by sport organizations, and they contribute to the decision-making process, which is a rare arrangement in comparison to other industries or sectors. At the same time, many principles or definitions of governance concepts may be the same or very similar, but it is the application, or practice of those principles that change in different contexts. In our experience of educating a variety of groups in and outside of sport, on governance, from governance professionals, nonprofit clubs and organizations, sport federations, as well as undergraduate and graduate students across the globe, we have learned that the practical application of governance principles in sport has particular challenges because of the historical context and development of sport and the cultural, historical context of sport organizations, and the people within those organizations. Therefore, to facilitate learning about sport governance, it helps to recognize context and how it influences our adoption or resistance to governance and the change it facilitates in sport organizations. As we mentioned many times (rather deliberately), sport organizations are complex, and at different stages of adopting good governance principles. We recognize this and incorporate contextual examples throughout the book to illustrate that building good governance in sport take time for learning, reflecting, evaluating in order to create genuine and beneficial change for, ideally and hopefully, all stakeholder groups. While "good governance" principles may be the same, or at least similar, around the globe, how we apply them and when, may need to be different in each sport organization. Sport organizations cannot go from no governance to full compliant with all desirable governance principles in the blink of an eye. By considering our own contexts and development, we can identify current capacities and potential resistance to changing governance, increasing governance. Careful implementation and evaluation of governance change can result in positive impacts, deep understanding of impacts of governance as well as improvements in the performance of sport organizations. Governance implementation or change that is not careful, sensitive to current capacities and historical context of sport organizations, can be frustrating and often fail, becoming a "tick box" exercise of compliance with funding agencies (such as governments) with little genuine change in values and performance of the organization.

With these little remarks in mind, "On your Mark, Get Set, Go!"

2 What Is Sport Governance?

Introduction

In its simplest form, sport governance refers to how decisions are made within sport organizations and, more broadly, how sport organizations control and direct operations. Decision-making and control should be fair, transparent, and equitable across the organization. This can be difficult to achieve given the growing complexity of many sport organizations and the environments in which they operate. There are also more complex aspects of sport governance that should be understood, such as the difference between governance and management, the implications of poor governance, and how sport governance can mean different things to different stakeholders. This chapter defines sport governance, its evolution, and complexities in order to provide readers with a clear picture of sport governance and its importance.

Since the turn of the century, sport, in all its forms, has evolved rapidly. At the highest level of athletic performance, we find that major sporting events attract hundreds of thousands of spectators, while millions of viewers are glued to their televisions and smart devices to watch unique sporting performances. Government funding of elite sport continues to rise across the globe and grassroots sport is a growing subsector delivered by the private, public, and voluntary sectors. Commercial aspects of all sport are growing exponentially, including betting and gambling, sponsorship, competitions, athlete branding, and events. There is no doubt that these activities generate significant revenues to a set of both commercial and nonprofit organizations from different industries. Unfortunately, the rapid expansion of sport, coupled with the shift in values from amateur to commercial activities, has also resulted in heightened attention from the media, exposing abuse, scandals, corruption, and other unethical behavior in sport organizations around the world.

DOI: 10.4324/9781003254324-2

The commercialization of sport has undoubtedly helped to mobilize the interest of many citizens to get involved in sports at all levels: local, national, or even international in volunteering, governance, spectating, and active participation. Sport has largely been managed autonomously in that, within national/international legal systems, sport has coordinated its own rules and structures to regulate stakeholders (athletes, administrators, etc.), but the legitimacy of sport organizations – both at the national and international level – seems to be increasingly questioned, largely due to the many examples of illegal and immoral behaviors of the same stakeholders, such as athletes, administrators, and coaches.

Governance as a subject of research and administrative practice is of particular value because it helps us to become more aware of (a) the social, political, and economic role of sport organizations in modern society, and (b) the consequences of governance failure or absence. In the simplest forms of organization of sport, such as sports clubs, the conditions are created in order for *the bond of common interest to exist*, as a vital part of what we call *"civil society."* These organizations are a common concern of their members and of all those citizens who choose to be activated in their functions, in order to produce benefits for their athletes and to design the so-called "models of development" of each sport. However, for this *common bond of interest* to thrive, a vision, strategic objectives, resources, clear policies, and control procedures are needed to ensure that legality is respected and that there is effective accountability and transparency. In this context, sport organizations must safeguard and strengthen the democratic processes within them. At the same time, it is essential that the respective leaders of sport organizations not only exercise effective governance in the current circumstances, but also work, care for, and ensure the smooth delivery of the *"baton"* to the new leaders, in the same way as the great athletes withdraw from the podium so that the younger ones can climb. When governance is absent or "diseased" at the national and international levels, then opacity, mismanagement of resources, and all kinds of scandals that erode the democratic processes that the organizations themselves have institutionalized, will prevail. At the same time, a significant lack of legitimacy challenges the autonomy and the interrelated right of self-regulation of sports organizations that, until today, have been taken for granted.

Autonomy and Legitimacy in Sport

Understanding "autonomy" and "legitimacy" in sport is important in order to understand sport governance and why it is important. Autonomy in sport means that sport organizations make their own rules, regulate competitions and leagues, and manage rule violations through systems of sanctions or punishment. The organizations (such as clubs and federations) that serve sport enjoy a unique autonomy based on its role and social characteristics. This role refers to sports perceived ability to contribute to social issues such as health, education, social inclusion, and culture, which has granted sport organizations the timeless right to self-organize, self-govern, and, by extension, to self-regulate.

Sport presents several special characteristics that make it stand out from other social goods and business activities. On this basis, this book draws from Chappelet's (2010)[1] definition of "autonomy" in sport, which is clarified as follows:

Always within the framework of national, European, and international law, the autonomy of sport is defined as the possibility of non-governmental, nonprofit sports organizations to:

1 Adopt, amend, and interpret regulations appropriate to their sport without undue political or economic influence.
2 They shall choose their administrative leaders democratically, without interference from States or third parties.
3 They shall receive adequate resources from public or other sources, without disproportionate obligations.
4 They shall use these resources to achieve objectives and continue their selected activities without external constraints.
5 They shall draw up, in consultation and consultation with public authorities, legal standards commensurate with the achievement of those objectives.

Autonomy is a fundamental condition for a modern sport organization. However, the maintenance of autonomy depends on whether the sport organizations that enjoy it are considered "legitimate." Once an organization is legitimate (well, of course, *achieving* and *remaining* legitimate is a constant exercise), it has proven its social suitability and therefore enjoys social support and has more room to do its job seamlessly. In the absence of legitimacy, however, autonomy is being challenged and undermined, which is why we also must clarify the concept of "legitimacy" and its importance in the sports ecosystem.

Legitimacy increases the acceptance and understanding of a sport organization and its actions by society, and at the same time contributes to ensuring sport's autonomy. Legitimacy ensures the stability of the organization, both in the internal environment and in its relations with actors in the external environment, which ultimately contributes greatly to its survival.[2] The logical question is then: "Why is legitimacy important to society?" The answer to this question is: "Because it makes the organization predictable, therefore safe, and thus worthy of trust."[3]

In recent years, however, many sport organizations have faced a "legitimacy gap" due to repeated scandals related to issues of corruption, human rights violations, mismanagement and oversight, which has called their autonomy and ability to self-govern into question. In essence, what is causing this "legitimacy gap" within sport organizations is that they (with some glaring exceptions) have not been able to adequately cope with the challenges brought about by the increasing commercialization and the resulting complexity of sport, which is reflected in the quality of governance of the sport organizations themselves.

The concept of legitimacy can be defined as a "social situation that can be attributed to an individual or action" and which is "recognized as good, appropriate or commendable by a group of third parties."[4] In other words, for an organization to be legitimate, it must also be perceived as legitimate by important external groups and the wider society; that is, it must also be *considered* legitimate.

The above approach stresses the importance of the dual aspect of legitimacy (i.e., being legitimate and being considered legitimate) to substantiate whether an organization is legitimate. Therefore, the recognition of the legitimacy of an organization by society can also be considered as a form of social control, in the sense that, in this way, society pushes the organization into practices, "services," and "products" that are expected to be judged as positive and useful by society itself. Thus, the legitimacy of an organization gives it the freedom to shape itself as it wishes. It therefore has the ability to shape its structures, as it wishes, and to produce "products or services" as it wants them. In the case of sport, both "services" and "products" are relatively well known. What is particularly important, however, is that the "public" in sport has a wide range of stakeholders that make it an autonomous institution. However, the paradox is that if a sport organization lacks legitimacy, this does not necessarily mean that it is an organization without fans and an affected public.

To sum up, organizational legitimacy is a field of study that can be understood from an institutional and a strategic angle. The institutional approach focuses on how organizations gain legitimacy through the stability of characteristics that are widely accepted. In the language of "sport governance," such organizational characteristics can be codified around concepts such as accountability and self-regulation, democratic processes, transparency, as well as societal responsibility. Under this approach, the main concern of an organization is to meet the expectations of groups and actors of its external environment. Therefore, organizational legitimacy is described as "a continuous and often unconscious process of adaptation, in which the organization reacts to external expectations."[5] For example, more and more people expect sport organizations to demonstrate their environmental awareness in the planning and implementation of sporting events; the latter, in turn, are timidly trying to meet these expectations, but the effectiveness of their actions is considered inadequate.

On the other hand, the strategic approach treats legitimacy as an operational resource, which an organization tries to extract, sometimes competitively, from its environment in order to achieve its objectives.[6] For example, a sport organization that is considered to be legitimate will attract more sponsors (and perhaps easier), because sponsors will prefer partnerships with highly legitimate organizations over collaborating with organizations whose legitimacy is being questioned, because the latter entails increased business risk.

Unpacking Sport Governance

The English term "governance," derived from the Latin word *gubernatio*, means that "someone guides/steers." In its simplest form, governance is ensuring compliance with relevant regulations and legislation to facilitate an organization's performance.[7]

Modern governance has evolved into a much more complex and multifaceted function performed by boards of directors, to ensure the legitimacy of sports organizations at both national and international level. In general, what we call "sport governance" means nothing more than the exercise and application of governance in the context and environment of sport.[8] In a more detailed definition of "sport governance," Ferkins, Shilbury, and McDonald (2009, p. 245)[9] stated that:

> *Sport governance is the responsibility for the operation and overall direction of the organization. It is a necessary and institutionalized component of every sporting entity, from clubs to national bodies, government agencies, sports service organizations and professional teams around the world.*

The concept of governance can be easily confused with "management," and the two concepts do indeed overlap. While governance is primarily a function of the board of directors (in voluntary positions), to set policy, identify the values, mission, and vision of the sport organization and ensure transparency and equity through the implementation of those policies/plans, management is the responsibility of the executive (see final chapter), often paid staff, to ensure implementation. However, the concept of management encompasses many interrelated concepts relevant to the function of organizations, such as culture, conflict, change, strategy, leadership, control, power/politics, and individual/group behavior.[10] Therefore, management is both a function of sport organizations, responsible for the day-to-day operations and implementation of governance policy and it is a wider field of study that can help to understand how boards/governance operate within the sport organization. Sport organizations are also complex systems of varying structures, cultures, environments, and human behavior, within which governance and management occur. It is beyond the scope of this book to cover all aspects of organizations, governance, and management, but recognizing these three concepts' distinctions and relationships can help the practicing manager to coordinate responsibility and avoid role conflict. Byers et al. (2015)[11] suggest that understanding control as a multilevel concept that involves organizational components (such as structures and human interaction) can help move understanding of governance beyond just that of policy development and compliance to a more dynamic process of negotiation that changes over time. This important relationship between governance and control means that sport organizations need to evaluate current governance systems and structures (from different stakeholder perspectives), to identify how changes to the existing governance can and should happen. This requires continuous communication, with a diverse group of stakeholders to understand past, current, and future governance needs.

Governance in sport: What's so special?

In essence, the question is this: What difference does this book offer from another that deals with corporate governance or the governance of *non-sports* nonprofits? The UK's National Code of Good Governance for Sport and Leisure lists four reasons/features that make governance in the field of sport a separate and unique process.

- Governance beyond the sports organization itself
  "Sport governance" encompasses many of the usual features of governance, such as vision, strategy, the effective functioning

of an organization, responsibility, and supervision. However, it extends to other important aspects, such as policies for the protection of children and vulnerable social groups, as well as to diversity, inclusion, and equality that contribute to the effective functioning of the organization and the wider sports ecosystem. While "sport governance" includes regulatory procedures, it also delves deeper into ethical processes. It also extends to procedures aimed at ensuring the effective and fair management and development of each sport, beyond the organization that serves it. In other words, the governance of sport goes beyond the supervision of an organization (structure) and extends to its better management of the sport and the environment, within which the sports organization operates to facilitate "fair play" and equity in sport competition and participation. In this sense, sport governance is a lively and multilevel process that is practiced not only by the leaders, but also "experienced" by the participants of any sporting activity and not limited simply to those who are members of a sport organization. Therefore, "sport governance" is a leading process that creates, maintains, and improves the structure of the environment, in which sport in its broader form, but also each sport separately, is cultivated and developed.

- The voice of the participants

    The sport sector is unique because athletes and participants in sporting activities are not just a category of stakeholders, but are the very focus of "service," especially in professional sport. Therefore, the "governance" of a sport organization must constantly and effectively recognize the central role of the athlete and the participants. For example, three important issues related to the "voice of the participants" should receive particular attention:

    - The form of participation of athletes and participants in decision-making.
    - The promotion and protection of athletes and the rights of participants at all levels.
    - The management of the dual career of athletes, as well as the provision for professional rehabilitation, at the end of the athletic career.

- The role of athletes as "heroes" and "ambassadors" of sports

    Another feature of governance that makes the sport sector unique is the active participation of current and former athletes of recognized value and influence in the promotion and development of the sport, who serve or have served in the past. Sport organizations often want (and should) honor and include experienced athletes in their promotional activities, but also in their other activities. How this can be achieved in the clearest and most constructive way is something that is of constant concern to sport governance.

• The passion of the volunteers
  One of the unique and very powerful features of sport is that its success depends, to a large extent, on working passion[12] and the dedication of volunteers, primarily locally, but also in many cases, internationally. Even in sport structures that rely on paid individuals, the work of volunteers is vital, although their enormous contribution to the development of sport is often underestimated. For this reason, sport, as a whole, is considered one of the most powerful and representative examples of the effective functioning of the Society of Citizens.

Levels of governance in sport

Drawing inspiration from sociopolitical economics,[13] Henry and Lee (2004)[14] understood and analyzed the term "governance of sport" through three levels: the systemic, the organizational, and the political. These three levels of governance, discussed below, are interlinked in that each affects the other and together they make up a conceptual framework of sport governance.

Systemic governance

The level of systemic governance is related to the form of competition (athletes or teams), cooperation, and mutual adaptation between sport organizations with other organizations from the wider sport ecosystem, including businesses and political institutions.

Systemic governance underlines the nature of a key change – on the one hand, in the way sport is organized, and on the other, in the way it is controlled. In fact, national governments are no longer just one of the factors that influence, decide, and control sporting events. This change partly reflects the globalized trends in sport and highlights the complex process regarding the organization of all types of sporting events (from the Olympic Games and national football championships to a local triathlon event). Therefore, modern sport is one of the most characteristic examples of a complex system, which is characterized by the constant interaction of organizations and other interest groups that work and operate both inside and outside these organizations.

If we become aware of the role of the various stakeholders, such as the media, event sponsors, sports sponsors, athlete agents, large clubs/companies and shareholders with a strong influence in business policy circles, it is easy to see that today's sport is an increasingly complex activity. In essence, systemic governance argues that decision-making is no longer a matter for an authorized body (such as an international sports federation), but a collective matter for a large number of cooperating organizations.

Systemic Governance in practice: Tokyo 2020 Olympic Games

The postponement of the Tokyo 2020 Olympic Games due to the COVID-19 pandemic is a prime example of understanding systemic governance, both at the organizational level and at the level of influence of different decision-making stakeholders.

During the 124 years of their history, the modern Olympic Games have only been cancelled in times of war: in 1916 (World War I) and in 1940 and 1944 (World War II). However, these three cases are not related to systemic governance as we are discussing in this chapter. In contrast to the above three cases, where the procedures were less complex, that of "Tokyo 2020" automatically created a huge "domino effect" in world sports and even in the required changes in the dates of many major events of all sports.

In March 2020, the Athens-Macedonian News Agency (ANA-MPA) vividly described the organizational difficulties as well as the financial cost (the organization of the games would reach 12 billion euros) that would have to be borne by a plethora of interested parties. Initially, the first calculation of the cycles of the Japanese economy spoke of huge economic damage, which would cost the "Land of the Rising Sun" approximately EUR 5.4 billion. Of course, the financial cost due to the postponement of the Games did not concern only and exclusively the host country. The International Olympic Committee (IOC) itself has also estimated that it will be financially affected by the postponement of the Games, with the result that it has spent some EUR 763 million of its "reserve" to support international sports federations and National Olympic Committees. According to English media, the British Olympic Committee stated that it had secured grants amounting to EUR 60 million and because of the postponement of the games it will resort to the British Government for funding to support both the preparation of British athletes and the viability of the Commission itself.

However, the systemic environment in which decisions had to be made complicated the situation even more. This was because England's insurance circles said the IOC had already spent approximately EUR

21.8 million to insure most of the investment of EUR 872 million that is "drawn" from the organization of every summer Olympic Games. The same circles even pointed out that the big insurance companies in London (to which the IOC has been addressing all these years) have suffered a "blow" that may have exceeded EUR 1 billion. To this whole picture should be added the claims of hundreds of millions from broadcasters, advertising agencies, sponsors, and hotels.

That being said, Japan was trying to delay the decision by arguing that the rate of outbreak of COVID-19 in Tokyo was much lower than in the rest of eastern Asia and Europe. The IOC, which was initially willing to wait until the end of May 2020, also seemed to want delaying the process before making its final decision. At the same time, many of the Olympic Committees of the traditional forces of sport, the European Federation of elite athletes, but also – individually – high-profile athletes (including the candidate for the IOC Athletes' Committee, Greek Olympic gold medalist and world pole vault champion, Katerina Stefanidi) expressed their misgivings about whether the Games should take place. At the same time, several countries (such as Canada and Spain) began announcing that they would not send athletes to Tokyo if the Games took place in the summer of 2020, in the midst of a pandemic.

Two additional factors further complicated this decision. The first concerned the tickets purchased for the Games (by December 2019, approximately EUR 653 million had been paid to purchase most of the seven million available tickets), an issue on which neither the Tokyo 2020 Organizing Committee nor the IOC seem to have had a clear position at the time. The second factor concerned the qualifying events that would send athletes and teams to the races, with only 60 percent of the series completed by the spring of 2020. This fact required readjustment of all planning (which is not easy), and close cooperation and coordination (perhaps even concessions) between the IOC and the international federations of dozens of sports.

It is understandable that the IOC was slow to announce a clear decision on staging the Tokyo 2020 Games. As it is understood, the mostly hierarchical model of governance of sport that prevailed until the early 1980s has given way to a complex web of interdependencies between stakeholders who wield power in different ways and in different contexts, forging alliances with other stakeholders inside or outside the web. Although each sport has its own specific stakeholders who exert pressure and influence processes for how competitions and leagues are organized, systemic governance generally involves various institutions, bodies, and organizations.

Systemic governance has at least three major implications for the organization and management of sport organizations, as well as sporting events:

- Initially, in a systemic environment any significant change affecting sports events can only be achieved through negotiations and/or exchanges between different parties in the network.
- As a direct consequence of the above, any governing bodies of sport (confederations, national federations, athletes' associations, etc.) and their representatives are unable to fully control their sport and, if this happens, it is due to the ability of these executives to negotiate their positions and not to dictate them to passive receivers.
- This means that people who work (voluntarily or otherwise) in sport organizations are required to firstly have negotiation and mutual adaptation skills and, secondly, have strategic thinking and the ability to plan, discuss, and communicate with a diversity of stakeholders.

In conclusion, systemic governance refers to what is, for the most part, a horizontal organization of mutually dependent actors in the wider sport ecosystem, of which only one is the State, which exercises imperfect control. From the perspective of systemic governance, then, the oldest linear top-down decision-making model does not exist. In essence, this framework lacks a clear hierarchy, as the correlations between sport institutions and organizations are constantly being negotiated. In other words, the governance of sport organizations based on the systemic level describes a model characterized by forms of cooperation, co-decision, co-determination and combined action that transcend, or even cancel out, all sorts of borders.

Political governance

Political governance is about the way in which the State – and the government or its organs – "steers" through regulation and incitement (and not through the exercise of direct control), the operation and behavior of sport organizations. At the beginning of this chapter, we discussed the concept of "autonomy" in sport, and in particular the freedom of sport organizations to organize themselves, to govern themselves, and thus to regulate themselves. Yet, while sport has the potential to regulate itself, it is faced with constant threats and serious challenges, such as the exploitation of young players, doping, racism, violence, corruption, illegal betting, and money laundering.

The above challenges have led governments to take a more active role over the last 15 years or so in the indirect governance of autonomous sport organizations. Since sport is a complex and important social and economic phenomenon that affects the strategic objectives of the States, the States themselves often seem to take initiatives aimed at directing and indirectly controlling the operation of sport organizations, while claiming to respect the autonomy of sport. Tools used by national governments to achieve their political objectives with regard to sport usually take the form of moral pressure or a threat of regulation that practically translates into "leverage of funding." It is worth noting that in recent years the European Union has also recognized the specificities and importance of sport and has made recommendations in the first instance to address the above challenges.

Political Governance in Practice "CHILON": Evaluating the Greek Sport Federations

Source: General Secretariat of Sports, February 2020

On February 19, 2020, the political leadership of Greek Sports, namely the Deputy Ministry of Sports and the General Secretariat of Sports (GSGA), officially presented to the sport community the CHILON evaluation system. CHILON, which bears the name of the Lacedaemonian sage of antiquity, is a multi-criteria evaluation system of the 48 sport federations and has a dual objective. On the one hand, it concerns the existence of a measurable and as objective as possible evaluation of the federations, which will be linked to the state subsidy. On the other hand, it is about providing clear information to the federations regarding what they should emphasize and where they should direct their resources.

The evaluation is based on 64 indicators collected from the data of the federations themselves and is based on an internationally and widely used methodology for similar evaluation cases, such as the international ranking for universities or countries in terms of the competitiveness index composed of many subindices (Global Competitiveness Index). These indicators constitute a multi-criteria analysis process with four dimensions or criteria: size, activity, athletic success, and governance. The performance of the federations, based on the various indicators and criteria, is determined by some reference values extracted from the sample of the federations compared to each other.

The weighting factors of the indicators and criteria are those parameters that determine the policy or direction that the State wants to give. The *size* is mainly determined by the number of sports, clubs, and active athletes and the history of each federation. The *activity* concerns internal competitions, development, national teams, the undertaking of international competitions, training and anti-doping activities, and finally the geographical coverage. The athletic success of each federation in the last two Olympic events and World and European Championships of all ages are taken into account. The procedure for scoring the athletic success follows the corresponding philosophy of the Hellenic Olympic Committee (each position depending on the organization and the age category gets similar grades). The athletic successes also include an element of Olympic heritage based on the participation of sports in the last ten Olympic Games. Finally, the criterion of *governance* takes into account elements of transparency (publications, either on the federation's website or in the national system, of decisions, minutes, and financial statements), the degree of compliance with good practices, the securing of sponsorships, the ratio of administrative costs to the total budget and the reduction of debts.

According to the secretary-general of the GSGA, Dr. Mavrotas, in 2020, 20 percent of the EUR 17.3 million in State funding was to be distributed according to the CHILON system; this percentage is predicted to reach 45 percent in 2021 and 70 percent in 2022. The ultimate goal of benchmarking between federations with the CHILON system is for the federations, in cooperation with the State through the interactive process, to accelerate the process of improving sport services to society. It is predicted that because this reform effort is governed by transparency and objectivity, it will bring positive benefits for the wider sport ecosystem of the country. In the words of the Deputy Minister of Sports, Mr. Avgenakis, *"Every grant will cease to be a matter of acquired speed, sympathy and acquaintances, and will now be the result of a global evaluation, both competitive and administrative."*

Government influence on the governance of sport is also well established in the United Kingdom, with good governance a requirement for funded sport organizations. The more funding received from government, the more evidence or sophistication required of the sport organization to demonstrate the principles of good governance. The Canadian government announced in July 2022, that they will be moving to a system of mandatory governance practices linked to funding for sport organizations across the country, in order to ensure safe and equitable sport provision.

Organizational governance

Organizational governance deals with regulatory and ethical standards of administrative behavior; in other words, it concerns, first of all, the work of the board of directors of an individual sport organization and the methods, institutional rules, and procedures through which this is achieved.[15] As a system of governance, the board is a mechanism of primary importance, because its main responsibility is to ensure that the actions of the sport organization are drawn up in the best interests of the organization, its members, and society. Good organizational governance has no goal other than to enhance the sustainability and effectiveness of the organization, both in the present and the future. High-organizational efficiency is important, but not at all costs. When (good) governance practices are sidelined in the pursuit of short-term high goals, this can harm the long-term viability of a sport organization.

In a recent handbook dedicated to the governance of sport organizations, the editors[16] pointed out that organizational and systemic governance have monopolized the interest of researchers in recent years. Indeed, concepts such as leadership (common, collective, authentic); the roles (as well as their ambiguity) and responsibilities of board members; the conflicts (interests) between them; cohesion and trust; power and gender dynamics within the board are some of the issues that fall within the level of organizational governance. Reflecting the trend of international literature, this book will focus primarily on issues and practices related to organizational governance.

Good governance is inextricably linked to organizational governance and, by extension, to business ethics. This is because it introduces specific bureaucratic practices, rules, and procedures.[17] However, practices, rules, and procedures that are identified with "good governance" are often considered appropriate, simply because they are widely applied or because they are expectations or requirements of other factors within the "organizational field." In other words, they are considered legal and ethical, not necessarily because they lead to higher organizational and athletic performance (i.e., increase in revenue, a larger number of members, the provision of more services to members and at the same time the emergence of more champions and/or champion teams), but because they are modern and supported by other members of the organizational field. Thus, the position of the authors of the present book is that bureaucratic practices, rules, and procedures are considered "good governance" when they have a positive impact on legitimation and effectiveness, while at the same time erecting effective obstacles to immoral and opaque behavior and practices. In other words, the application of rules of good governance at organizational level should not be an end in itself, but the *means* to achieve good governance.

Conclusion

This chapter asked the question: "What is Sport Governance?" Governance in sport is broadly about decision-making and ensuring transparent and responsible management of sport. More specifically, sport governance can be understood through three levels, with each demanding policy-making so that there is efficiency and effectiveness in the wider sport ecosystem. Systemic governance stresses the need for mutual adaptation between the different parties or organizations involved in the production of sport. For example, a sport's governing bodies can no longer simply impose their will without negotiating with the other stakeholders and organizations. Political governance then emphasizes the guidance of governments through political interference rather than through direct and direct control, which undermines the right to autonomy enjoyed by sport organizations. Finally, organizational governance is a normative approach that requires sport organizations to meet the broader social expectations of good practice, which in turn has an impact on the management of such organizations. Therefore, each of the three levels of governance entails challenges in the traditional form of administration, management, and policy of sport organizations. They now need not only flexibility to cope with an ever-changing sport environment, but also a wider range of skills and abilities, to maintain the necessary legitimacy and maximize their effectiveness in all aspects of their operation. Sport governance is also largely relevant to the many unique aspects of sport discussed in this chapter including the increasing recognition of stakeholder voices, the role of volunteers and paid professionals, the passion and commitment felt by those working in and participating in sport. In short, sport governance is complex and sport organizations should not underestimate this complexity but seek to learn about the many levels, perspectives, and histories of governance in their own organizations. They should also seek to challenge existing practices and ask if governance can be improved so that the sport organization can be more diverse, inclusive, and professional in delivering sport, developing sport, and creating a positive impact in society through sport. Sport governance is also part of the wider concept of management which has formal, tangible elements that are created by, challenged, and changed by individuals and groups. Good governance in sport ensures that individuals and groups are not advantaged or disadvantaged but that decisions taken in the organization are for the benefit of all stakeholders, fair and equitable. Rules and policies designed to ensure the ethical practice within the sport should be followed and/or developed and evaluated for impact.

Notes

1 Chappelet, J. L. (2010). L'autonomie du sport en Europe. Council of Europe.
2 Suchman, M. C. (1995). Managing legitimacy: Strategic and institutional approaches. Academy of Management Review, 20(3), 571–610.
3 Stamelos, G. (2014). The issue of social legitimacy of Greek universities: Historical origins, future challenges (1974–present) (full text in Greek). Academia, 4(1), 200–236.
4 Coleman, K. P. (2007). International organisations and peace enforcement: The politics of international legitimacy (p. 20). Cambridge: Cambridge University Press.
5 Palazzo, G. & Scherer, A. G. (2006). Corporate legitimacy as deliberation: A communicative framework. Journal of Business Ethics, 66(1), 71–88.
6 Suchman, M. C. (1995). Managing legitimacy: Strategic and institutional approaches. Academy of Management Review, 20(3), 571–610.
7 Shilbury, D. & Ferkins, L. (2020). An overview of sport governance scholarship. In D. Shilbury & L. Ferkins (Eds.). Routledge Handbook of Sport Governance (pp. 3–17). Oxon: Routledge.
8 Hoye, R. & Cuskelly, G. (2007). Sport Governance. Oxford: Elsevier.
9 Ferkins, L., Shilbury, D. & McDonald, G. (2009). Board involvement in strategy: Advancing the governance of sport organizations. Journal of Sport Management, 23, 245–277.
10 Slack, T., Byers, T. & Thurston, A. J. (2021). Understanding sport organizations. Champaign, IL: Human Kinetics.
11 Byers, T., Anagnostopoulos, C. & Brooke-Holmes, G. (2015). Understanding control in nonprofit organisations: Moving governance research forward? Corporate Governance: The International Journal of Business in Society, 15(1), 134–145.
12 Anagnostopoulos, C., Winand, M. & Papadimitriou, D. (2016). Passion in the workplace: Empirical insights from team sport organizations. European Sport Management Quarterly, 16(4), 385–412.
13 Specifically the work of Leftwich, A. (1994). Governance, the state and the politics of development. Development and Change, 25(2), 363–386.
14 Henry, I. & Lee, P. C. (2004). Governance and ethics in sport. In S. Chadwick & J. Beech (Eds.). The Business of Sport Management (pp. 25–42). Harlow: Pearson Education.
15 Hoye, R. & Cuskelly, G. (2007). Sport Governance. Oxford: Elsevier.
16 Shilbury, D. & Ferkins, L. (2020). An overview of sport governance scholarship. In D. Shilbury & L. Ferkins (Eds.). Routledge Handbook of Sport Governance (pp. 3–17). Oxon: Routledge.
17 Geeraert, A. (Ed.) (2018). National Sport Governance Observer. Final report. Aarhus: Play the Game: Danish Institute for Sports Studies.

3   How Do Boards in Sport Behave?

Introduction

In this chapter we introduce the different theoretical approaches that have contributed to the understanding of the multidimensional nature and complexity of organizational governance. It is common knowledge that the literature has no dominant theory of governance in the field of nonprofit organizations, let alone sports organizations. Researchers occasionally plan their research with reference to different theoretical approaches, which makes it difficult to compare results and draw widely accepted conclusions about governance. Therefore, in the relevant literature we will encounter different theoretical approaches to organizational governance, some of which may conflict with each other. The focus in this book is on the ways in which sports organizations construct governance or are shaped by it. Therefore, the choice of the theories of governance to be cited in this chapter was made solely on the basis of the practice of governance. We have chosen to present the most important theoretical pillars of the relevant literature, which attempt to interpret the content of governance and provide initial answers to some of the *"whys"* of the practices that we find today in the governance of smaller and larger sports organizations.

In this chapter, we list and analyze the basic assumptions of eight governance theories with the aim of highlighting central governance issues, such as the dynamic relationship between the members of the General Assembly and the elected board of directors (hereinafter referred to as the "board") (see *"agency theory"*); the management of uncertainty inherent in the dependencies of organizations to secure resources (see *"resource dependency theory"*); the complexity of the targeting of needs by different interest groups (see *"stakeholder theory"*); or the coexistence/cooperation of the board with the salaried administrative staff (see *"stewardship theory"*).

DOI: 10.4324/9781003254324-3

Theoretical Approaches to Governance

Agency theory

The *agency theory* approaches the concept of "sport governance" by focusing on the relationship between those who make up the General Assembly of a sport organization ("principals") – that is, active members – and those who are called upon to exercise leadership and management ("agents") in the day-to-day operation of the organization. The basic principles of the agency theory are:

- The members (principals) choose to entrust, after an election or another procedure, to a group of executives (agents) the management of the sport organization for the members' benefit.
- Agency is related to the relationship between the members and the elected/appointed administration.
- The cost of agency is borne by the members who elect the administration and involves monitoring the performance of the elected and controlling their behavior.
- The assumption of the duties of the administration by the members implies the obligation to be accountable to the members they are called to serve.
- The logical hypothesis of the theory is that the principal will provide a small or greater degree of freedom of action to the agent, who may respectively choose to either work hard or flee.

The agency theory argues that it is possible for the members of a sport organization to have different interests from those of, for example, the executives that the members themselves elect for the management of the organization and prefers that it is the interests of the members that should dominate the decisions of the executives for the operation of the sport organization. Essentially, according to this theory, in a situation where different interests exist between the parties, the principal will try to limit such conduct on the part of the agent that essentially limits the achievement of the objectives of the former. In other words, on one hand, the existence of a control mechanism for the agent is required in order to prevent unacceptable behavior, and on the other hand a mechanism of incentives, so that the behavior of the agent produces benefits for the principal.

This theory is one of the most basic approaches to the study of sport governance because it focuses on identifying all those measures or mechanisms that will enable members to effectively supervise the administrative acts of elected members, to their advantage. It also draws the attention of members to the demand for quality and timely information in order to be able to judge whether and to what extent elected or appointed directors act with a view to the well-being of the members. Therefore, the basic aim of the theory is to identify those conditions and mechanisms that will enable members to achieve their goals and meet their needs, through the assignment of the responsibilities of the organization's management to representatives.

In the context of a sport organization, we can come across different examples of representation, such as:

- The relationship between the members (i.e., clubs) and the elected board members.
- The relationship between the elected volunteer board members and the paid director(s) of the sport organization (e.g., the CEO).
- The relationship between the financier (state, sponsors, etc.) and the board of the funded sport organization.
- The relationship between important interest groups (such as high-performance athletes, players) and the leadership of the professional team.
- The relationship between the CEO and the other paid administrative staff.

The main obstacles to the application of the above theory to sport organizations are the ambiguity that characterizes these organizations in terms of who is the main principal. For example, in sports clubs we could assume that the principal is the founding or the informed members, but the athletes also rightfully claim a place in the teams of the principals. In the case of federations, we could assume that the principals are the active member clubs; however, other stakeholders with reasonable claims from the operation of these organizations should also be considered, such as athletes or coaches. When reference is again made to legal entities (such as public sporting facilities), the assignors can join a set of stakeholders that request and receive access to the use of these facilities, such as the municipality and its citizens.

Overall, this theoretical approach highlights the need the board to have strict control over the actions and behavior of the paid administrative staff, especially of the CEO (in those cases a sport organization has one). For for-profit sport organizations that have shareholders, this theory is applied to study how well a system of governance works. In the case of nonprofit sport organizations, however, the theory's implementation is rather limited, partly because the element of profit is lacking and partly because the primary objective is to satisfy different interest groups.[1] Practically then, agency theory highlights how the unique attribute of sport governance to be inclusive of a wide range of stakeholders creates a challenge to have clear communication and prepare for regular change as ideas, criticisms, or demands are exchanged and processed through the decision-making structures.

Stewardship theory

The starting point of the *stewardship theory* is the human relations[2] that are developed within sport organizations and this theory is placed in the opposite direction of the agency theory. The main difference between the theories is that the stewardship theory recognizes other motives for the actions of paid executives, beyond those of economic self-interest. It suggests that there is no conflict of interest between agents and principles (e.g., between the board and the member-club or between the CEO and the board members) and that, in order to enhance the effectiveness of a sport organization, an appropriate structure is required so that coordination is carried out in a more efficient way.

The centrality of this approach, then, is that paid senior management has as their primary concern to be productive in their work and thus also to act as caretakers of the organizational resources available to sport organizations, because, as management professionals, their only motives are the need for higher performance, taking responsibility, recognizing, and, above all, respecting the hierarchy and not maximizing their personal benefits at the expense of the other stakeholder groups of a sport organization. Therefore, the members and, above all, the elected board of a sport organization can be seen as an important partner of the paid administrative staff, whose role does not focus on constantly monitoring the compliance of these administrators, but on jointly improving the performance of the organization.

In this theory, the role of the board is limited to the design of the strategy and the close cooperation with the paid management – mainly with the CEO – in order to successfully implement its decisions. Therefore, it is understood that the members of the board should be selected on the basis of their expertise (with a level of diversity to capture a broad range of knowledge and skills) and the interfaces they contribute to the organization, in order to contribute with sound decisions. This implies that the board and the CEO have sufficient training and comprehensive information communicated to be able to function effectively as a team, with some optimal level of conflict, that serves to enhance decision-making and performance.

Managerial hegemony theory

The *managerial hegemony theory* argues that the organizational structures, the structures of power transfer, control, and supervision have essentially languished or have reduced efficiency, which has led to the dominance and hegemony of the paid administrators/executives. Indeed, crises aimed at the behavior of the board of sport organizations and originating mainly from within can be interpreted from the perspective of managerial hegemony theory. At the heart of this theory is the actual distribution of power and control in a sport organization. Let us not lose sight of the fact that, in recent years, the operation of many sport organizations has been in the hands of paid administrators/executives who, due to their daily professional involvement with the organization, inevitably gain control of it. A look at the largest international sport federations will show us that they are run daily by powerful executive directors (CEOs) who have significant training and experience in handling complex issues and challenges.

The hegemony of management refers to those cases of organizations where the board acts as a mechanism for the simple validation of strategic decisions (rubber stamp),[3] which are essentially taken by paid administrators/executives. This approach stresses that these executives have the precedence and readiness to exercise control of an organization over board members.[4] This theory highlights two central governance issues:

1 The separation of those who participate in the "ownership" of the organization from those who ultimately control its day-to-day operation, and
2 The continuous professionalization of sport organizations as tools for development and sustainability, which is faced with the inevitable challenge of aligning itself with boards that are unpaid and composed of volunteers.

Stakeholder theory

The stakeholder theory is based on the assumption that nonprofit sport organizations should take care of the well-being of different groups in society and not be limited to their members alone.[5] In this sense, the organization is perceived as a set of relationships and responsibilities toward more recipients, which also directly affects the governance model.

This theoretical approach brings to the fore the requirement (or need) that sport organizations be able to manage a significant number of relationships with different stakeholders, such as member-clubs, affiliated organizations, athletes, coaches, referees, paid administrative staff, sponsors, facility managers, suppliers, and others. From the above, it seems that the goal of governance can only be to maximize the value offered to the specific stakeholders that contribute to the sustainability of the sport organization and it is natural to claim benefits from its operation.

In contrast to the traditional approach of the management of sport organizations, this theory highlights the need for new skills at the level of the board and paid staff of sport organizations, which will approach and convince various stakeholder groups to work together for a common mission in conditions of interdependence. In this regard, Salamon (2001) noted that the board requires certain skills, such as:

- Activation, to reach out to groups that can help solve serious and chronic organizational problems.
- Orchestration (diplomacy, communication, negotiation, etc.) so that all diverse stakeholder groups work together harmoniously.
- Coordination and harmonization of relations to ensure control and balance in the network of relations in question.

Resource dependency theory

The *theory of resource dependence*[6] is the first of three theories that focuses on the external environment of sport organizations. It analyzes their governance by exploring the interdependencies that govern their operation and concern the influx of resources from their environment. The economic and functional survival of most sport organizations is in the hands of other organizations or groups, who finance their actions indirectly or directly. These may include public bodies that finance sport or provide access to facilities, beneficiaries purchasing sports services, sponsors concluding agreements for marketing purposes, international federations providing the regulatory framework of sports and related leagues, and others.

The above dependencies require effective management methods in order for each organization to ensure the uninterrupted flow of resources and information required for its operation. The role of the board is considered very important because it is the main mechanism available to the organization in order to control its insecurity and build influential relationships in the external environment, thus securing valuable resources. One of the main functions of the board is to maintain harmonious relations with important external bodies and to work to ensure a seamless inflow of resources into the sport organization.

The management of resource dependencies requires the board to carefully monitor changes in the sport environment (which can be stable at times and dynamic or rapid at other times) and to ensure that the organization constantly evolves and adapts in order to more effectively serve its mission and the main groups of beneficiaries, such as athletes and its respective members. Sport organizations can accomplish this through their own environmental monitoring but often benefit from seeking outside perspectives from community, academic partnerships, or consultants. This theory forces us to study and evaluate the extent to which the board acts as the catalyst in the organization's struggle to acquire the necessary links to secure significant resources, not just financial ones. For example, the board may provide the organization with legitimacy, counseling, collaborations with other organizations, support for obtaining valuable information, securing technological resources, or other important resources.

In administrative terminology, this role of the board is also known as the "boundary-spanning mechanism" of the sport organization and requires its members to have the necessary knowledge, skills, and connections in both the sports and the wider social environment. For example, several sports clubs depend on municipalities for their access to sports facilities and they often push their representatives to participate in local councils and committees to strengthen their bargaining power to their advantage.

Institutional theory

Institutional theory still concerns an approach that regards the external environment as the central core of the exercise of governance. According to the neo-institutionalists,[7] organizations within the same organizational field tend to evolve similarly to each other, always according to the imposed limitations in their behavior. In other words, in every field (including sport), organizations are now homogenized; that is, they are very similar in the way they seek resources, in the way they structure their internal functions, in the way they serve their stakeholders, and, therefore, in the way they show dysfunctions.

The concept that defines this process of homogeneity is called "institutional isomorphism."[8] It is an invisible process of limitation that affects/forces a large group of organizations to exhibit many common characteristics in terms of its behavior, because they face the same environmental conditions. Isomorphism is developed through three mechanisms: coercive, normative, and mimetic pressures.

Coercive isomorphism comes from formal rules – that is, laws and interrelated penalties – and ensures the compliance of organizations. In other words, these are action arrangements that are established by the state or other important supervisory bodies (such as the IOC, international sports federations, WADA), and are binding on all sport organizations that are part of the regulatory framework of influence.

Normative isomorphism is the result of ethics and behavioral patterns disseminated through educational institutions and through the dissemination of information to professional and business networks, in conjunction with the rules and techniques adopted in the organizational field. In other words, it concerns ethical pressures, stemming from specific codes of professional conduct.

Mimetic isomorphism emerges from the social expectations associated with imitating the behavior of other organizations in terms of success or leadership. In other words, it is the tendency of an organization to imitate others who have already successfully solved problems that another organization is facing for the first time. An example of such mimetic pressure is the recently developed Code of Good Governance for national sports federations of the Republic of Cyprus, which drew inspiration from similar established codes of various countries around the world, such as Belgium (Flemish), New Zealand, Australia, and Great Britain, while taking into account the particularities of the Cypriot environment.

All in all, the neo-institutionalists claim that, due to the above-mentioned pressures, the organizations of a field tend to become increasingly similar to each other. Moreover, any organization that has incorporated institutional elements from its immediate environment retains them for a relatively long time because it understands that they contribute to its sustainability. However, like any theory, the institutional one – which is a deterministic approach – does not help us to understand how intra-organizational conflicts and inter-organizational competition contribute to organizational change. Put it differently, while the neo-institutionalists described isomorphic compulsion, they did not record the innermost mechanisms through which it is possible to exercise this compulsive isomorphism. In any case, institutional theory is useful for understanding the reasons that explain why several boards of sports organizations operate in a similar way and incorporate comparable practices and governance structures.

Theory of democratic governance

The principles of Western democracy are an integral part of the governance of sport organizations and are often clearly reflected in their founding statutes. According to Cornforth (2003), the central ideas of democratic governance are:

- Free elections on the basis that each member has the right to one vote.
- Representation; that is, the elected members of the board represent the interests of the electors and not of the electors themselves.
- Accountability to the electors.
- A clear distinction between the elected officials who design policies and those who implement decisions.

Democratic principles and interrelated practices have significantly influenced the governance of a large majority of nonprofit sport organizations. This is because their starting point is the members, who, according to the statutes of these organizations, are called to elect the board that will represent their needs and values and will develop the mission, strategies, and programs of the organization.

The *theory of democratic governance* puts forward that the board's mission is to represent the expectations of the members and not the elected board member themselves. This principle is intertwined with the statutory provision of nonprofit sport organizations, which safeguards the right to vote and stand for election to every member of the organization. In recent years, however, there has been an accumulation of knowledge and research data, which shows that the basic principles of democratic governance mentioned above do not seem to produce governance practices of sport organizations characterized by efficiency, transparency, and accountability.[9] In large sport organizations, in the absence of specialization in the board, serious governance problems often arise, linked to unlawful administrative actions and scandals. These problems directly call into question the commitment of the organization and its leaders to the mission, which is none other than the satisfaction of the needs and expectations of the athletes.

Effective democratic governance requires the training of all cooperating stakeholder groups in order to enhance their systematic information and participation in meaningful consultations and processes that produce mature and realistic policies for sport organizations. The aim is an organizational culture that will affirm the needs of the

beneficiaries against the voice of those involved in the management of
sport organizations.

Conclusion

These theories attempt to enhance the understanding of the concept
of "governance" at two levels.[10] At the first level, the focus is on the
day-to-day management of different stakeholder groups. At this level,
paid administrative staff choose to exercise governance "playing on
the basis of existing rules." The second level focuses on the will to
overturn the existing governance correlations and to redesign the
institutional conditions for governance with the ultimate aim of focusing on new needs and interests.

By way of summary, two elements should be highlighted:

1   The evolution in organizational governance in sport is a global
reality and is therefore a complex area of study that involves legal,
cultural, and other structural variations. Therefore, some theories
may be more appropriate in some countries than in others or more
relevant at different times depending on the stage of development
of governance in which a country or group of countries finds
itself. The development of governance within sport organizations
can be attributed to sports history and culture, the development
of the economy, the legal framework, and the educational level
of those involved, all of which can influence how governance can
evolve and be harmonized within the country.

2   All the above arise and derive theoretical substance from a different field each time. For example, "agency theory" originates from
the fields of finance and economics, while "stakeholder theory" is
based on a viewpoint oriented mainly to social groups. Although
there are significant differences between theoretical approaches,
as each one attempts to analyze the same problems from different
perspectives, they also share many commonalities.

As highlighted in Chapters 1 and 2, we can see that diversity/inclusion,
communication, and change are central themes in understanding governance, even from different theoretical perspectives. The focus of this
chapter, behavior within the board, reveals that change may be initi-
ated from within the board or from external stakeholders, and requires
constant monitoring and management. This includes recognizing that
increasing the diversity of a sport board will have an impact on communication and will improve decision-making capacity because of the

increased breath of knowledge and skills of board members. Change within the board (such as increasing diversity) will change the dynamics and nature of interaction – with perhaps some conflict initially – while new perspectives are voiced and challenge existing ways of operation. However, change is healthy and good for all organizations, breathing new life and ideas, giving new people opportunities to contribute and to benefit from inclusion in sport governance. The theories presented in this chapter are meant to help sport managers and sport governance professionals to recognize that there is more than one way to understand behavior within a sport board. As such, often times, it is helpful to reflect on current behavior and practices to identify alternative modes or possibilities for improving the performance of the board, be that through communication methods, diversity of the board or other changes identified as potentially beneficial to the goals of the sport organization and its governance processes and mechanisms.

Notes

1 Hoye, R. & Cuskelly, G. (2007). Sport Governance. Oxford, UK: Elsevier.
2 Muth, M. M. & Donaldson, L. (1998). Stewardship theory and board structure: A contingency approach. Corporate Governance, 6(1), 5–28.
3 Hung, H. (1998). A typology of theories of the roles of governing boards. Corporate Governance, 6(2), 101–111.
4 Lorsch, J. W. & MacIver, E. (1989). Pawns or potentates: The reality of America's corporate boards. Boston, MA: Harvard Business School Press.
5 Hung, H. (1998). A typology of theories of the roles of governing boards. Corporate Governance, 6(2), 101–111.
6 Pfeffer, J. & Salancik, G. (1978). The external control of organizations: A resource dependence perspective. New York, NY: Harper & Row.
7 See, for example, DiMaggio, P. J. & Powell, W. W. (1991). The New Institutionalism in Organizational Analysis (Vol. 17). Chicago, IL: University of Chicago Press.
8 Ibid.
9 Kihl, L., Kikulis, L. M. & Thibault, L. (2007). A deliberative democratic approach to athlete-centred sport: The dynamics of administrative and communicative power. European Sport Management Quarterly, 7(1), 1–30.
10 Chhotray, V. & Stoker, G. (2009). Governance Theory and Practice: A Cross-disciplinary Approach. London, UK: Palgrave Macmillan.

4 Inside the Sport Boardroom
What's the Score?

Introduction

The main responsibility of sport organizations – local, national, or international – is to set goals and design policies and rules that support the development and promotion of sport and expand its popularity. The objectives can only be achieved through effective governance, which ensures the application of basic principles such as democracy, equal opportunities, accountability, independence, and transparency. Therefore, the concept of sport governance implies roles with interlinked responsibilities and tasks, leading to objectives, strategies, and individual policies, producing results for beneficiaries and important stakeholder groups. We all expect strategic objectives and policies to be communicated efficiently and effectively so that the governance of the sport organization is transparent, inclusive, ensures accountability, and is based on democratic, informed processes.[1]

The Board of Directors

A key element of sport governance is the empowerment of individuals to lead sport organizations, make decisions, supervise, and, at times, enforce compliance of behavior with transparent rules and procedures. For example, the president of a sport federation is responsible for preparing the agenda of the meeting(s) that will lead to important sport-related and financially-related decisions. In this case, governance determines the tools by which the exercise of power and supervision in a sport organization is carried out. In other words, governance includes the responsibility of elected or appointed members to shape the proper functioning and monitor the performance of the sport organization. The board of directors ("the board") is responsible for ensuring that the individual strategies, policies, and

DOI: 10.4324/9781003254324-4

actions of the organization meet specific criteria (such as being fit for purpose, equitable, and non-discriminatory) and conditions, as well as produce benefits.

But how can we ensure the board has legitimacy to lead a sport organization in this manner? This responsibility and power are rooted in the approved statutes of the sport organization, which is the so-called *"Blueprint"* of its operation. The statutes reflect the mission of the sport organization and describe the main governance structures (general assembly, board of directors, permanent committees, etc.), as well as the conditions for their establishment. Essentially, powers and authority are delegated according to the statutes, but the board must hold those to whom it is delegated to account (member clubs and their athletes, coaches, volunteers, etc.).[2] The basic governance structures of the organization do not change often because the process of changing the statutes is relatively complex, time-consuming, and requires a lot of negotiation.

The statutes of the largest sport organizations are framed by the internal regulations and other regulatory texts (such as regulation of high-performance sport, incentives to reward athletes and coaches, and evaluation of clubs) that list the individual sport policies and regulate the daily operation of the organization. The term "policies" is used to describe individual and detailed regulatory frameworks that are voted on/approved by the board to manage issues in a consistent and transparent way such as:

- Selection of athletes for the staffing of the various national teams.
- High-performance sport incentives, awards, and other relevant issues of athletes' motivation.
- Recruitment of coaches or other managers.
- Claiming or awarding championships.
- Operating costs.
- Membership.

Forms of boards of directors

The boards of sport organizations are not all the same based on a number of parameters. We encounter significant differences based on factors such as the way members are selected, the number of members, and the roles they play.[3] The selection of the members of the board of a sport organization has a significant impact on the way it operates, but also on the strategic priorities that its members will set during their term of office. Therefore, it is directly identified with the quality and effectiveness of the organization's governance. In sport, we identify three types of boards: elected, appointed, and hybrid.

Elected boards: The members of the board of a local sport club or a sport federation are elected from the base of the members of the clubs of that specific sport (or discipline). The statutes provide for specific elections for the selection of the board, which are described in detail and must be kept to the letter. However, the process of elections should also obey the articles of the relevant national legislation.

Depending on the national framework in which a sport organization is included, board elections can be an open process with candidates organizing an election campaign to claim a seat on the board. However, in some cases the sport organization establishes the Nomination Committee for the board, which proposes, checks, and approves the nominations so that they meet certain criteria when participating in elections of a sport organization.

Elected boards: These boards have the maximum legitimacy to run a sport organization and are therefore guardians of the independence and autonomy of sport organizations. However, remember that the election process involves enough uncertainty to ensure that elected members actually have the skills required to exercise quality leadership and cooperate harmoniously with the rest of the administrative and technical staff of a sport organization.

Appointed boards: Some boards of sport organizations are selected by existing members of the board, who propose new members after evaluating them and after documenting that they meet statutory criteria listed in the statute.

Unlike elected boards, appointed boards seem to contribute more to maintaining stability within the sport organization, because they either stay longer in their positions (longer terms) or more effectively reflect continuity in leadership. This is because legislation and political culture encourage the selection of new members who share common values and views with the departing members. This can lead to stagnation in the development of the organization or sport as there is little change in board members, there is little change in capacities, skills, and experience.

Hybrid boards: In recent years, we have seen international sport organizations and federations that choose to be governed by hybrid boards, in the sense that some of their members are elected and some appointed or participate in the board because they have special knowledge or hold an important position in another important organization (ex officio). Some of these members may have a seat on the board without the right to vote. For example, according to recent changes to the statutes of the World Anti-Doping Agency (WADA), the president and vice-president will be appointed on a proposal from the Nomination Committee, which will have thoroughly checked their independence from national sport organizations and federations.

In many international federations today, it is foreseen that athletes will participate in the boards as regular members with the right to vote or in an honorary position without the right to vote. An indicative example is the World Triathlon Federation, whose board includes two athletes, namely the chairperson and vice-president of the Athletes' Committee, who were elected by athletes (ITU, 2020). Something similar is happening in the World Boxing Federation, where provision is made for the participation in the board with the right to vote of an athlete, who has been elected by the Athletes' Committee (AIVA, 2018).

Hybrid sport boards have the advantage of combining the positive elements that meet in elected and appointed boards. Elected members ensure the ability of the sport organization to better meet the needs and expectations of its members, while appointed members seem to contribute more frequently to the stability, independence, and sustainability of the sport organization.[4] They may also provide important representation of an important group of stakeholders directly impacted by board decisions. However, we should not lose sight of the fact that hybrid boards also carry the risk of provocation or malfunctions. If some of the elected and appointed members disagree on the priorities of the sport organization, it can be difficult to make important decisions. For the appointed members, the dedication to the sport organization and its mission may not be evident, as in the case of elected members. When the participation of appointed members is due to a contractual obligation, it is possible that their motivations to offer time and expertise in board matters may fluctuate.

Independence of Board Members

The independence of members when participating in boards is an important parameter for improving the governance of sport organizations, primarily through reducing conflict of interest. However, the process of selecting members of sport boards cannot fully ensure their independence or eliminate any conflict of interest. The Australian Institute of Sport (2015) argued that all members of the board of a sport organization must be independent, and this cannot be guaranteed by their selection process alone (i.e., whether they are elected or appointed). To this end, the Institute proposed four criteria that constitute evidence of the board members' independence: (a) they are not elected by the members representing a particular interest group, (b) they have no employment relationship with the organization, (c) they do not hold any other position within the organization, and (d) there is no conflict of interest between their membership and any status that results from their other occupations.

Therefore, members who sit on two parallel boards of national federations or who are employees of public bodies and have also been elected to federations or local associations cannot be considered to act independently in their capacity as members of sport organization boards. Of course, there are exceptions, such as those of international federations which have established specific conditions, so that only members of the boards of national federations have the right to stand as a candidate on their board. In such cases, it is necessary to redefine how the members of the board document their independence.

An interesting example of this is New Zealand Cricket, which revised its statutes in 2013 to select board members in two phases. The first phase involves an open call for tenders and evaluation of the candidates by an independent committee, while in the second phase the members of the assembly elect the board from the candidates proposed by the independent commission (Bradbury & O'Boyle, 2015).

So, What Do the Boards Do?

A metaphor can help explain something that is unclear/unknown by comparing it to something more familiar. If we use a boat metaphor for a sport organization,[5] boards can make two distinct types of action: steering and rowing.

- When steering, the board collectively:
  - Sets the direction of the organization.
  - Determines which values and logic will guide it.
  - Ensures the organization's resources are used prudently to advance its work.

- When rowing, board members expand the organization's resources, individually or collectively, by means such as:
  - Offering pro bono professional services or expertise to management.
  - Volunteering as frontline service providers.
  - Advocating for or championing the organization and its mission in the community.
  - Helping to raise funds to sustain the organization's work.

Modes of Governance for the Board

Effective governance of sport organizations is a complex process because it involves and concerns several groups that often have different interests and needs. We can include athletes, coaches, technical and medical staff, the media, fans, sponsors, teachers, volunteers, and even parents in these groups. In order to meet the expectations of the benefiting teams, the work of the board members regarding the governance of sport organizations must be not only important but also targeted. Therefore, governance is only possible when the roles and, above all, the responsibilities of the members of the board are clear and well defined.

In today's complex sporting ecosystem, leaders are required to work in multiple modes; similarly, boards are required to govern in multiple modes.[6] In their seminal and highly influential work, Chait, Ryan, and Taylor (2005) proposed three modes of governance: fiduciary governance, strategic governance, and generative governance. Together, these three modes of leadership constitute different but complementary aspects of the board's governance responsibilities. Figure 4.1 is adapted from "governance as leadership" framework and provides a condensed view of the implications to governance practice of the three modes.

In the fiduciary mode (Type I), a board's primary focus is stewardship of tangible assets congruent with the organization's mission.

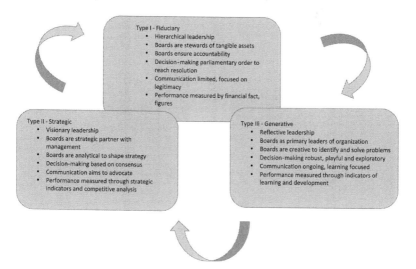

Figure 4.1 Three modes of governance: Practical implications.[7]

Fiduciary roles include financial oversight, legal oversight, risk management, and compliance with relevant legislation. This mode of governance can be understood when considering three types of responsibilities the members of the board have:[8]

- The obligation to take care means that the member of the board assumes responsibility for the careful supervision of the financial transactions of the organization and also for coordinating the individual activities and ensuring the viability and development of the sport organization. Therefore, members of the board who do not participate in the meetings are not aware of the minutes and may vote for proposals without knowing their content; they are in breach of the specific obligation that they have as members of the board and thus offer the organization low-quality leadership and governance.
- The obligation of loyalty refers to the obligation of the members of the board to put the interests of the sport organization above their individual or other business interests. This means that members may not take advantage of their position on the board to obtain financial or other benefits for themselves or their business or to obtain preferential treatment for their children or relatives in relation to various sporting matters. In several cases, for example, board members of sport organizations have been brought to justice, either because they misused the organization's financial resources or because they participated in illegal transactions to serve their interests.
- The obligation to respect the law requires each member of the board to ensure that the operation of the sport organization is in accordance with the applicable legislation and that the respective decisions and activities of the board are fully aligned with the mission, statutes, and other regulations of the organization. The supervision of compliance with the law is usually quite self-evident for board members, but vigilance about the organization's mission and objectives is more complex. The responsibility for overseeing legality is intertwined with the obligation of board members to account for the observance of legality, financial viability, and the overall performance of the sport organization.

A board's primary focus in the strategic mode (Type II) is to ensure that the organization possesses a robust strategy. A board functions as a strategic partner with management. The strategic mode involves the establishment of the strategic directions and priorities of the organization. The board must also guide and supervise the organization in order to implement actions and activities that will lead to the successful implementation of the strategic objectives. One of the most important strategic objectives of nonprofit sport organizations is the creation of resources to finance their sport activities and the promotion of the sport. The board's contribution is necessary not only so the organization gains access to necessary resources, but also to effectively manage existing resources by following specific and transparent policies and procedures. The board is also responsible for developing cooperative relations with other organizations or interest groups, with the aim of achieving the organization's goals. A sport organization is indirectly or directly dependent on other local or national bodies for the implementation of its sport programs and the promotion of the sport it cultivates in the wider society. The board is also responsible for the promotion and enhancement of the image of the sport organization in the wider society and partners. The board selects or approves the messages and content of external communication and is therefore entirely responsible for fostering a positive image in society. Also, since communication is not limited to messages or publications, but is also expressed in behavior, the members of the board have the responsibility to act as ambassadors in the way they carry out their tasks and represent the organization on a daily basis. Moreover, the board is responsible for anticipating the risks that the organization faces in a timely manner, to assess the risks and, with the help of salaried staff, to develop specific risk management plans, which are regularly updated and evaluated for their efficiency. Examples of risks may be accidents in sport competitions or championships, or cancellations of championships due to public health problems. Just as importantly, the board is responsible for evaluating the effectiveness of the work and the contribution of the board itself as the top governance body of the sport organization.

Finally, the generative mode (Type III) is least familiar to board members, and not just to those members of sport organizations. In this mode, the board functions as a sense-maker mechanism and provides leadership accordingly. The generative mode is largely a cognitive process where boards analyze complex, ambiguous, and/ or controversial issues. For example, will adherence to principles of good governance improve the organization's performance? Will greater diversity inside the board bring better results on the field? In this mode, boards focus on the organization's purpose, question assumptions, and discern the core values that advance strategic and tactical decisions. In doing so, different framings of the matter/issue in question become available, which determines decisions. In the generative mode, questions may include the following: How should we think about issues facing our organization? Are we focused on the right problem? What opportunities, challenges, and issues do we face? Where do our mission and core values come into play? How will various stakeholders view this decision?[9]

There is no doubt that all modes of governance are important and each has its own value. Without Type I, governance is meaningless. Any organization that fails to fulfill its fiduciary obligations will go "out of business." However, merely ticking boxes and ensuring that no wrongdoings occur does not mean that the sport organization is effective, or even relative for that matter. Thus, Type II is also crucial, as through this mode the board sets the scene, prioritizes activities, and deploys the necessary resources. However, Type III maximizes the value of governance (more generally) as well as the value of the board members themselves (more specifically).

Conclusion

This chapter has identified that the board, in its leadership of sport governance, has a number of different responsibilities, which may be approached by boards through different forms: elected, appointed, and hybrid boards. The use of hybrid boards is increasingly proving effective for sport organizations trying to adapt to a constantly changing sport landscape and remain representative of their membership. Whichever form is used to form the board, the independence of individuals on the board is essential to the operation and governance of the sport organization. Independence means that board members prioritize the organization's needs over any personal gains or objectives and do not profit from their position on the board. This is particularly important when we consider the different modes of governance that indicate boards must be responsible for the finances and resources of the organizations (fiduciary mode), for the strategic and long-term viability of the organization (strategic mode), and for the more abstract issues and challenges, values, and assumptions (generative mode) that drive the board. The generative mode requires creative, critical thinking and evaluation of board performance and reflection in an unbiased, self-critical manner. Ask yourself "what's the score?" with regard to which modes of governance your board (or a board which serves you as a stakeholder) exhibits. Which modes need strengthening and how can this education be actioned to provide useful training and development to the board?

In reflecting on modes of governance, the three themes of this book continue to be relevant. For instance, modes indicate a "collective" responsibility of the sport board and clear communication and discussion is needed to reach consensus as an organization, on policies, public relations, or external understanding of the compliance of members to the policies set by the board. Diverse sport boards are generally thought to be more creative and resourceful, but this can also require more communication and resources to reach a collective decision. Nonetheless, the goals of sport boards should be for the benefit of the sport, not individual boards members and so thinking of modes of collective action is essential.

Notes

1 Thompson, A., Lachance, E., Parent, M. & Hoye, R. (2022). A systemic review of governance principles in sport. European Sport Management Quarterly. [online first] https://doi.org/10.1080/16184742.2022.2077795
2 Bennet, Carpenter & Wilson, 2018.
3 Hoye, R. & Cuskelly, G. (2007). Sport Governance. Sydney: Elsevier.
4 Worth, M. J. (2012). Nonprofit Management: Principles and Practice. (2nd Ed.). London: Sage.
5 Ryan, P. W. (2008). Distinguishing a Board's Steering and Rowing Work. Briefing Note. Available to the first author through the Executive course 'Mobilizing your Board', Harvard Kennedy School. May 2021.
6 Trower, C. A. (2013). The Practitioner's Guide to Governance as Leadership: Building High-performing Nonprofit Boards. San Francisco, CA: Jossey-Bass.
7 Adapted from Governance as leadership: Reframing the work of nonprofit boards by R.P. Chait, W. P. Ryan & B. E Taylor. Copyright 2005 (p. 7) by John Wiley & Sons, Inc.
8 Worth, M. J. (2012). Nonprofit Management: Principles and Practice. (2nd Ed.). London: Sage.
9 Trower, C. A. (2013). The Practitioner's Guide to Governance as Leadership: Building High-Performing Nonprofit Boards. San Francisco, CA: Jossey-Bass.

5 Sport Board Composition
Who's Making up the Board?

Introduction

In theory, the mission and strategic objectives of sport organizations shape their internal structure and leadership. The structure and composition of the board should reflect those strategic objectives, and the board should be composed of members with specific skills and knowledge to contribute to the organization achieving its mission and vision. As sport organizations are dynamic and changing in response to internal and external environment pressures, changes in board composition can be healthy for the sport organization if it requires new ideas, knowledge, skills, or perspectives. In this chapter, the board is considered as a dynamic and responsive component of the sport organization. Because the board is a key decision-making mechanism, the question of who is on the board greatly affects how those decisions are made and the impact they have on the sport organization's effectiveness. Of course, many sport clubs are born as small, social, and informal with few rules, formal structures, or bureaucratic processes. As the organization grows, through attracting more members, organizing more events or training, the board should also grow in size and diversity in order to accommodate the growing membership and activities. Without change and growth, sport clubs can become insular and only serve an elite or select group, failing to make a meaningful social contribution to their respective community. Without a growth in governance knowledge, sport organizations are in danger of leading to social exclusion and reduced diversity in participation and volunteering which is a direct contradiction to the United Nations (UN) recognition of sport's ability to make a meaningful contribution to global sustainability and social cohesion. The UN set out, in its 2030 Agenda for Sustainable Development, the 17 areas of sustainability (e.g., women's rights, energy, peace, equality, conservation, etc....)

DOI: 10.4324/9781003254324-5

it sees evidence of and further potential for the power of sport to influ-ence. To achieve such high expectations, sport boards need the right people, with the right skills, experience, and desire to provide gov-ernance that facilitates sport's ability to reach more people, a greater diversity of people, and create quality experiences.

Sport Boards: The Decision-Making Mechanism

The boards of sport organizations make many decisions, all of which shape the organization, to varying degrees. Ideally, boards strive for quality in decision-making, in order to contribute to the effective operation of the organization in question. Board decisions affect the development of sport, the sustainability of organizations, and their ability to meet the needs and expectations of their members. Decision-making is a complex process, and while boards may strive to be objec-tive and gather all facts and information relevant to a decision, there are many factors that influence the decision-making of boards such as historical and social context, institutional norms, or conflicting agen-das, personal bias, and unconscious bias. However, understanding good governance and the role that decision-making plays is height-ened with understanding the composition of the board and how it may influence the sport organization.

Based on the statutes of a sport organization, the decision-making process normally belongs to its board, which is responsible for the overall supervision and control of the resources and activities of the organization. All this leads us to the assumption that sport boards are very important, so their performance depends directly on the skills and experience of their members. Let's examine in greater depth the process of composition of the board of sport organizations, to understand what factors affect its performance as a decision-making mechanism.

What Do We Mean by "Board Composition"?

The concept of board composition was introduced in recent years in the literature on sport governance to focus the debate on all those characteristics and parameters that should be taken into account when attracting and selecting members who form the board of a sport organization. Most of the statutes of the sport organizations refer mainly to the number of members, the duration of their term of office, and the way they are selected, which are usually the elections in the organization's General Assembly.

However, the experience of international sport organizations, combined with the recommendations of the supervisory bodies of countries around the world, have already broadened the relevant debate by including parameters such as attitudes, values, skills, and typical qualifications for members.[1] These parameters also include restrictions on the length of tenure, diversity based on gender, age, cultural identity, as well as proven evidence of the members' absence of conflict of loyalty or conflict of interest.

Why Is the Composition of the Board Important?

The composition of the board is important because the board's role is complex and requires multiple and varying skills, experience, and perspectives. The board is collectively responsible for developing/revising the mission of the organization, the strategic direction of the organization and the policies for the development of sport programs. Boards must also develop action plans for implementation, find the necessary resources, and periodically update the governance model of the organization so that it successfully focuses on goals and addresses challenges. All this can happen only when the board makes sound decisions, which depends directly on the skills and knowledge of its members. Therefore, it is necessary to have clear processes that define the conditions of composition that will lead to the selection of competent and experienced members with a willingness to offer their service to the sport organization.

A board that is composed of diverse skills and experience, gender, and race/ethnicity will be in a strong position to address strategic issues and collaborations with external bodies. It will, at the same time, be more ready to create and exploit opportunities in the external environment. The most realistic approach to the modern operation of sport organizations is the premise of being called to operate in a complex environment. In other words, boards are called upon to cooperate with various internal interest groups and external bodies (public agencies, international federations, municipal entities, sport facilities, sponsors, media, etc.). Therefore, the abilities of the members are very important for the effective management of all these relationships and interactions.

Boards may also require members with political skills to negotiate agreements that will bring about vital resources, build partnerships, and smooth out commitments from supervisory bodies that fund them and – most importantly – make rational decisions to allocate resources and meet strategic needs. All this leads to the conclusion that the decision-making process in the board is basically intellectual work, which requires both mental and technical skills.

We shouldn't lose sight of the fact that boards are projected to society as being representative of a sport and its members. Their elected and/or appointed members often possess a strong social profile in the local sport community and beyond. This means that their own behavior motivates and directly or indirectly influences the behavior of different stakeholders associated with the sport organization. Salaried administrative staff, coaches, volunteers, and even athletes (as well as their parents) receive messages from the behavior of board members and such messages are expected to be positive to help them integrate into the sport culture and embrace the ethical values of the organization.

What Skills Are Important for Board Members to Have?

The days of leadership and management of sport organizations being the privilege of a small number of people who held the positions for many decades are numbered. In the past, parents of athletes, former coaches, or local businesspeople put some of their free time toward supporting a sport board, but most sport organizations today need strong boards that can lead the organization and the sport to develop within a competitive environment. These organizations take this issue very seriously and describe not only the tasks of the board members, but also the skills and knowledge required to make a meaningful contribution to the leadership of the organization.

Therefore, the leaders of sport organizations are called upon to face complex problems and need knowledge and skills that enable them to:

- Allocate time and make an effort for the board.
- Be ethical individuals, communicative, and trustworthy as personalities.
- Be able to clearly articulate their thoughts and the vision they have for the sport and organization.
- Be willing to engage in continuous education to support the needs of the organization.

Board members may also assist with specific skills and experience in the organization's management issues. These abilities and skills include:

- Technical knowledge about the sport.
- Ability to develop strategic thinking.

- Communication, interpersonal, and teamwork skills.
- Business skills, such as economics, marketing, personnel management, and law.
- Close relations with the sport community to which the organization is addressed.
- Developing partnerships with organizations and individuals in the wider society.
- Ability to approach specific issues relating to minority groups such as women, people of diverse ethnic backgrounds, persons with a disability, etc.

The characteristics, knowledge, and skills of the board members should also complement each other. Below we examine some of the key parameters for achieving that.

Composition Parameters of the Board

Diversity

Several studies have shown that diversity is linked to the performance of the board and sport organization.[2] We know that boards with increased representation in terms of gender and skills are more effective, innovative, creative, and manifest an increased degree of dedication and cooperation. As such, sport organizations are encouraged to introduce changes to their statutes to enhance the diversity of their board and build inclusive and diverse memberships. A diverse board is more capable of addressing the complex and diverse environment that they face.

Notably, the 2016 Sport Governance Code in the United Kingdom provides that the largest sport organizations, with more than £1 million in public funding, should be governed by boards with proven diversity in terms of the skills, experience, knowledge, gender, and independence of each board member. Also, the board should systematically inform its members, as well as the state, about the required skills, experience, and knowledge of its members.

Recent studies on the importance of the diversity of boards have focused on the distinction between superficial and in-depth analysis of the diversity of a board.[3] A board meets the criterion of *superficial diversity* when its members differentiate from each other on the basis of mainly visible individual characteristics, such as age, gender, race, or other physical abilities. The superficial diversity of a team is useful for mitigating team reactions to avoiding stereotypes and for understanding the needs of individual sport teams.

However, *it is the deep diversity* of the board that can most often lead to positive reactions to the way in which a sport organization tries to respond better to the needs of its members, because when the board is diverse, it expresses itself through different attitudes, values, and opinions, which leads to the synthesis of better decisions, healthier collaborations, and creative conflicts. Increasing diversity in the board means that more pressure is applied to represent more social groups, both at the board level and at the level of the members of sport organizations.[4] Superficial diversity is achieved prior to deep diversity, which may take a longer period of time to achieve and evolves with diverse groups contributing to the organization.

Participation of women

In 2015, the Australian Sport Committee predicted that at least 40 percent of board members of sport federations would be women.[5] In England, the institutionalization of representation of both sexes (at least 30 percent) has led to a significant increase in women's representation.[6] Also, several international federations have already provided in their statutes for a gender-based quota (e.g., the board of the International Triathlon Federation is expected to have at least four members of either sex among its nine total members).

However, in most cases, national federations in many countries either do not make any mention of the issue or promise that they will attempt to ensure that there is female representation in the board and other statutory bodies. So, while the existence of intention should be recognized, in practice the intention itself does not change the landscape at all. There is no doubt that several sport organizations in different countries are resisting the introduction of a gender quota, which means that policies that will enhance gender equal access to sport leadership are absent from governance.[7] We argue that quotas are important because they lead boards to a gender balance and therefore build superficial diversity, which can lead to deep, more meaningful integration of different gender perspectives. After all, empirical studies have shown that gender diversity leads to better organizational performance, and the boards that have more gender equality tend to focus more on their mission.[8]

The counterargument is that the quota only helps the numerical increase of women (superficial diversity). Nothing ensures that women participate in decision-making and influence the priorities of a sport organization, so it is important that genuine practices of inclusion are continued to ensure women have a voice and consideration in decision-making. In addition to the quota, other measures are needed to gradually involve and strengthen women in sport governance structures. These include (a) the placement of women as members of the board in positions of responsibility, (b) the promotion of gender equality as an important organizational value, and (c) the promotion of cooperation and team spirit in the board.[9]

Participation of athletes

Sport organizations' compliance with the Western principles of good governance entail reforms that promote the participation of important stakeholders, which are affected by the operation of sport organizations (athletes, coaches, referees, etc.) in the activities and decisions of the organization. This is because an organization is effective when it can serve the needs of the most important stakeholders – and athletes are arguably among the most important stakeholder in the organization's mission. Although athletes are placed high on the strategic priorities of all sport organizations, this group has not always had a voice in the decision-making mechanisms.

So why should athletes have a strong voice on the boards of sport organizations? Firstly, their participation implies more effective policies and programs that meet the needs of the athletes themselves. Secondly, athletes are directly dependent on sport organizations to develop their sporting talent and the career they desire in sport. Therefore, the absence of votes and voices on the part of athletes makes it difficult to place the issues that concern them on the agenda of the board, which leads to decisions that are less effective. Thirdly, their participation in the decision-making process makes them participants in the design of policies and rules, so the implementation of these decisions can be more effective and efficient. There is less likely to be resistance to the policies if the athletes themselves are part of the policy development.

These are some of the reasons why it is important for athletes to have a voice on the board of a sport organization and to form the standing committee of athletes. Participation may be for active athletes or former athletes. The most important aspect of their involvement is that the governance of sport organizations will focus more emphatically on their needs and related policies and that they will be able to introduce accountability of board members and administrative personnel. Remember that the essence of representative democracy is for organizations to respond to the needs of the most important stakeholders in their mission, and that is none other than the athletes themselves. This is also a strategic and sustainable development tool for the education of potential future board members, which could be relevant when athletes are at the end of their performance careers.

In recent years, several international sport federations have amended their statutes to include athletes with the right to vote on the boards. Indicative examples are: (a) the International Tennis Federation, which provides for the participation of two athletes in the 14-member board (one man and one woman) and (b) the International Triathlon Federation, where the president and vice-president of the athletes' committee of the organization participate on the board.

Participation of independent members in the board

A good practice in sport governance is for the board to be composed of a number of independent members, although they do not have the right to vote. This practice is more applicable to large national federations and/or international federations. The importance of the presence of independent members on the board is multifaceted. Initially, they have the ability to enrich with specialized knowledge, the strategy of the sport organization. For example, a researcher-university professor, who does not come to the board of the national federation as a representative of one of the clubs of (any) sport, will be able to help in the theoretical approach and methodology of the preparation of strategic planning. In addition, independent members may convey to the sport organization the expectations of the wider society, and not only those stemming from the immediate environment of each sport served by the board (i.e., the member clubs).

Of course, the selection of independent members for the board must be made on the basis of criteria of prestige and recognition. At the same time, an external member must meet the following conditions:[10]

- Not have recently been a member of the board.
- Not have recently been employed in a senior executive position in the sport organization.
- Have no affinity with a board member.
- Not provide consulting, legal, or other services to the sport organization, either as a freelancer or through a company.
- Not be a supplier of sport equipment/material to the sport organization.
- Have been selected on the basis of a specific and transparent procedure.

Renewal and Term Limits of the Board Members

The issue of board renewal does not seem to have been of much concern to sport organizations, which often results in international sport organizations being in the spotlight of negative publicity for the procedures they follow regarding the staffing of the board, the long duration of the terms allowed, and the low representation of women on the boards.

However, planning and managing the renewal of the board is a strategic challenge for any sport organization that wants to fulfill its mission and vision.[11] The renewal process includes (a) planning and anticipating the skills and knowledge that the sport organization needs to achieve its goals and (b) the creation of a pool of individuals who can potentially take on important roles on the board of the sport organization.

The above issues highlight the need to remove some members to facilitate the renewal of the board. The regular renewal of the board entails significant benefits for the governance of the organization including new skills, innovations, management systems, and political connections. In the public debate, the renewal of the board is also intertwined with reforms to enhance transparency and the fight against corruption or complacency in sport organizations.

Therefore, the renewal of the boards is an important parameter of good governance and is implemented in practice by establishing restrictions on the number and duration of the terms of office of the members of the board. For example, the UK Sport Code of Governance (2016, 2021) provides for the commitment that each member is elected for two to four terms and remains on the board for no more than nine years in total. This is because we know that the long-term presence of a member in the leadership of the sport organization is often associated with an increased likelihood of re-election, a waste of resources to "buy out" support, uncertainty about the election of new candidates, recognizability, and excessive power.[12] Therefore, the limitation of terms of office can stop the concentration of power in some members and the use of that power to remain in place for long periods. Knowing that the length of their term of office is limited, members are more likely to focus on policies that will benefit the entire organization rather than specific stakeholders.

Although the setting of restrictions on the presence of members on the board seems to be gaining ground in international sport organizations, most national and local organizations do not yet recognize its usefulness. As expected, strong criticisms have questioned the introduction of measures to facilitate the renewal of the board. Taylor and Robinson (2019) summarized these reviews in four counterarguments:

- *"The renewal measures will lead to the board's loss of skills and knowledge."* This is a reasonable criticism of the sport organizations that have not yet drawn up specific renewal plans for their board and therefore do not have mechanisms to check its skills. The board should prepare and follow plans for its renewal to avoid losing important skills or this loss being replenished by the new members.
- *"Who will ultimately do the job?"* It is true that nonprofit sport organizations that rely on the services of volunteers/board members face significant problems in attracting and finding available and competent volunteers. But effective sport governance is intertwined with actions to attract talented volunteers who make up the pool of each sport organization, from which new members will emerge to *"do the job."*
- *"Renewal leads to the loss of people with prestige and influence, both at national and international levels."* The structure of sport internationally includes cases of members holding positions on more than one sport board (such as the national and international federations). These members are aware of the internal information of international federations and may have a favorable influence on decisions on various technical or organizational issues. This case requires statutory changes in the governance of sport organizations internationally, even though it only concerns a small number of members.
- *"Recycling of posts."* It is common practice for members to rotate in positions on the board to circumvent any restrictions provided for by the statute or the wider legal framework, or to achieve their election more easily. For example, a person may "run" as a candidate for the post of secretary-general when s/he has just completed her/his term as president. These are not actually open positions that aim to select new members for the board, but a cyclical rotation of existing members.

While boards may perceive difficulties in finding new board members, this is not always the case and an optimistic and positive, inclusive and welcoming policy on regular recruitment of new skills and experience is often met with interested volunteers. Contrary to what opponents of the institutionalization of specific terms in the boards have argued, it becomes evident that their renewal is an important process that helps improve the governance of the agencies. Although this is a complex process that requires careful handling, sport organizations must apply term limits for their board members. The criticisms that usually dominate the debate around the modernization of the governance model of sport organizations should not overshadow the significant benefits of renewing the board.

Conclusion

The composition of an effective board is one of the biggest challenges in the governance of sport organizations, and it requires procedures and policies that are regularly evaluated and updated to meet the modern needs of the organization. Today, many boards result from elections, while others combine elections with the appointment of members. Each process has positives and negatives. The board is responsible for assessing the "pros" and "cons" and for selecting the governance structure that leads to strong and effective leadership. Sport organizations are autonomous and independent and therefore have the means to systematically assess their governance structure and adapt it according to their needs. However, regardless of the governance structure, what should not escape us is that all board members should be held accountable for their performance and behavior at regular intervals, while the organization should be guided by a dynamic board. This chapter asked: "who is on the sport board?" The answer provided throughout the chapter indicates that board membership requires a diversity of people, skills, and experience and it is important to continuously evaluate if new people or skills may be needed – the disadvantages of change in board members is mitigated by the new ideas and fresh insights brought by embracing this change. Continuous change also encourages greater communication to ensure new ideas are thoroughly considered, and increasing the diversity of a sport board is something that also happens continuously, so it is never too late to examine a sport board composition and identify new skills, ethnicities, or gender need to improve decision-making.

Notes

1 Cunningham, G. B. (2016). Diversity and inclusion in sport organizations (3rd Ed.). London: Routledge.
2 Sotiriadou, P. & Pavlidis, A. (2020). Gender and diversity in sport governance. In D. Shilbury & L. Ferkins (Eds.). Routledge Handbook of Sport Governance (pp. 366–380). London: Routledge.

3 See, for example, Kerwin, S. & Doherty, A. (2019). Board dynamics in nonprofit sport organizations: Contemporary research directions. In M. Winand & C. Anagnostopoulos (Eds.). Research Handbook on Sport Governance (pp. 439–454). Cheltenham: Edward Elgar Publishing.

4 Buse, K., Bernstein, R. S. & Bilimoria, D. (2016). The influence of board diversity, board diversity policies and practices, and board inclusion behaviors on nonprofit governance practices. Journal of Business Ethics, 133(1), 179–191.

5 Australian Sport Commission (ASC) (2015). Mandatory Sport Governance Principles. Canberra, Australia.

6 Bennett, A., Carpenter, K. & Wilson, R. (2018). Sport Governance. ICSA, the Governance Institute. London: ICSA Publishing.

7 Adriaanse, J. & Schofield, T. (2014). The impact of gender quotas on gender equality in sport governance. Journal of Sport Management, 28(5), 485–497.

8 Harris, E. E. (2014). The impact of board diversity and expertise on nonprofit performance. Nonprofit Management & Leadership, 25(2).

9 Adriaanse, J. & Schofield, T. (2014). The impact of gender quotas on gender equality in sport governance. Journal of Sport Management, 28(5), 485–497.

10 Clarke, T. (1998). Corporate governance: An international review. Journal of Research on Corporate Governance, 6(1), 57–66.

11 Taylor, T. & McGraw, P. (2006). Exploring human resource management practices in nonprofit sport organizations. Sport Management Review, 9(3), 229–251.

12 Geeraert, A. (2015). Sport governance observer 2015. The legitimacy crisis in international sport governance. Copenhagen, October 2015.

6 The Strategic Governance Mode

What Does It Mean in Practice for Sport Organizations?

Introduction

Most sport organizations face indirect or direct competitive pressures in their efforts to attract funding, new athletes, sponsors, facilities, coaches, volunteers, and other important resources. While some people are under the impression that sport organizations are protected, the reality is that they must survive in an environment with many stakeholders, limited resources, and, above all, increasing uncertainties about the available support from public and private bodies. One of the priorities of governance is to identify the critical strategic issues facing a sport organization and to define these strategic priorities, objectives, and action plans that will support the sport organization's sustainability and development.

This chapter focuses on the strategic role of the board of directors (hereinafter referred to as the board) working with strategic planning as a guide. The board puts in place strategies that are guided by a clear vision and mission, thus helping the sport organization cope with uncertainties. At the same time, the board aims to identify, in a timely manner, the significant problems and challenges faced by the sport organization and then analyze them with a strategic approach and dedication to the realization of the vision. In essence, this chapter aims to transform the strategic mode of governance that the board exercises into its practical parts.

The Concept of "Strategic Governance"

The governance of the sport organization shall focus on the strategy and, above all, on the way in which the board, in cooperation with the executive management, prepares the strategic future of the organization. The strategic planning also includes vision, values, the mission,

DOI: 10.4324/9781003254324-6

policies, and, above all, the action plans (or programs) that will make it possible to implement the strategy. Therefore, strategic governance is intertwined with strategic leadership. This gives "governance" purpose and direction, toward a defined, achievable, long-term goal.

Strategic governance focuses on all those processes by which the management of a sport organization is put into practice at a strategic level, with the organization's long-term future in mind. The central concepts governing strategic governance are none other than leadership, power, accountability, transparency, and democratic processes. However, the implementation of these concepts is not self-evident or simple. It requires that specific practices and procedures are put in place that will lead the sport organization and its board to explore complex strategic dilemmas and decisions. Effective strategic governance distances the sport organization from the management of everyday life. It is important that sport organizations are flexible and put in place effective strategic governance practices. Let's look at some examples of such practices:

- The board and the executive management have articulated the mission, vision, and values of the sport organization clearly. This may require the board to examine their current versions of these and critically question if change is needed.
- The starting point for action for the sport organization remains the development or revision of a strategic plan, both in the daily planning and in the meetings of the board.
- The sport organization shall have clear action plans to achieve the objectives and results set out in the strategic plan.
- The measurement of efficiency is based on impacts, not only on outputs (inputs).
- The board is responsible for guiding the strategic direction of the sport organization and this is reflected in formal policies and documents.
- The work and discussions of the board – as well as its committees – focus mainly on strategic issues. Board members understand that they have a responsibility to focus their leadership role on strategic, long-term governance.

Strategic Thinking and Board

Consider two sport boards. The first has largely neat procedures for its operation. Its agenda is announced in good time and the meetings are short and comprehensive. Financial supervision is continuous and the sport organization in general operates satisfactorily until a strategic issue emerges. For example, the organization has been asked to participate in a multi-sport event that will be hosted in a city nearby. The board is then set up and, in the spirit of cooperation, tries to manage/ correct what is possible (i.e., more of a fiduciary mode of governance).

The second board operates completely differently. Its meetings are full of tension and controversy, but it focuses primarily on important long-term issues, such as improving athletic performance, acquiring new sources of revenue, and improving policies to manage important resources. Its members are mainly concerned with how to improve services to the athletes, the members of the organization, and the wider society. It is difficult to make decisions on these issues immediately, but such strategic issues have been raised in the board table for analysis and discussion (i.e., supporting a more generative mode of governance).

It is understood from the above two scenarios that the first board is concerned with short-to-medium-term issues, while the second is more often concerned with larger, long-term issues and therefore delves deeper into issues related to the needs of stakeholders. Undoubtedly, the second board devotes more time to important strategic and generative modes of governance, while the first gives more attention to elements that require timely attention and action. While we can refer to the differences between these boards in terms of their "modes of governance," another way to look at it is in the type of thinking each board exhibits.

The well-known theorist Peter Drucker[1] introduced the term "strategic thinking," aptly observing that "*the best way to predict the future is to create it yourself.*" But what does "strategic thinking" mean? It requires both critical thinking and long-term consideration of implications of current issues. Therefore, strategic thinking employs critical thinking on vital issues that either affect or will affect the efficiency, effectiveness, and sustainability of the sport organization, both in the near future and the long term. At the board level, strategic thinking guides its members to develop strategic planning on how to fulfill the organization's mission and better respond to the challenges of the modern, changing environment. Practically, this means that the adoption of strategic thinking at the level of the sport board is a routine activity followed with discipline and leads to tangible results in terms of the quality of decisions. Strategic thinking and strategic planning are related concepts that complement each other.

At the board level, *strategic thinking* is further defined in relation to whether its members:

- Thoughtfully upgrade the strategies and efficiency of the sport organization. In this case, they identify malfunctions or look for opportunities and ideas that will improve the strategic position of the organization, and carefully select the issues that they will delve into with a critical eye (see the example below: "Critical Thinking in action").
- Are consistent in the way they base their thoughts and decisions. In this case, they analyze complex issues in a systematic way and approach the major problems from different angles. They try to identify the real causes of the problems and to interpret the available information in different ways, so that they can be led to documented ones.

Given that strategic thinking requires recognition of complex issues, identification of potential solutions or directions and activities to be pursued by a sport organization, diversity in the board is essential to provide that broad range of perspectives and knowledge. The following is an example from consulting in a Canadian sport organization.

Strategic Thinking in action

A board of directors of a high participation sport, which is financially stable and has a clear strategic plan to continue to be a popular sport but to also grow participation in terms of diversity and inclusion, has identified a problem that occurred a couple of years ago when there was significant attrition in its elite program. This trend continued to be a challenge in terms of large numbers of drop-outs at elite levels. The board realized this could have serious long-term consequences for the sport organization, so it hired a consultant to investigate the reasons for the problem and to recommend solutions. The consultant identified an inefficient and political selection system for elite teams, fear and power differentials in parent – coach relationships, as well as conflict of interest throughout the selection process. The recommendation was to address this and make selection more objective. The sport organization completely redesigned its selection process, built anonymity into coach evaluation, and created a system that was more transparent and less subjective. They also began planning to evaluate their current board to broaden the skills and perspectives to better inform their decision-making generally.

When critical thinking dominates sport boards, their members are more willing to take the time and try to resolve the important issues.

It pleases them to discuss issues relating to institutional changes in the external environment, such as the needs and expectations of the members for upgraded sport services, competitive pressures in the sport market, etc. Their meetings focus on the important issues and lead to useful and beneficial decisions.

The board, as mentioned above, also recognized that although it had many strengths, there were still challenges within the organization and it contracted the same consultant to guide its strategic planning process, which it allowed to take place over 18 months of meetings and input to board development. This served to create a significant change in board capacity as the consultant challenged existing ways of thinking and brought new ideas for board structure and function for the next 5–19 years.

Why Should the Board Be Involved in the Strategy?

The board's substantial involvement in the development of the strategy brings many benefits to the sport organization.[2]

- The board understands the challenges of the external environment in which the sport organization is called upon to operate, as well as the internal capacities and resources at its disposal. Therefore, its members can contribute to discussions on the strategic issues.
- By participating in the development of the strategy, the members of the board adopt the strategy and are indirectly committed to serving it during the implementation phase.
- Board members propose different perspectives on the analysis of strategic issues, which improves the quality of strategic decisions.
- Strategic thinking encourages consultation of board members on alternative objectives and action plans, while strategic planning encourages board members to work harmoniously with executive staff to implement it.
- The board feels that it is fulfilling its role when its knowledge and skills bear fruit, resulting in the continuous improvement of the sport organization.
- The members of the board are more informed and act as defenders of the sport organization when they speak and promote in the external environment its strategic actions.

It is clear that strategy development requires extensive communication and discussion, both within the board and between the board and other stakeholders.

Board involvement in the development of strategic planning

While the role of the board in the development of the strategy is indisputable, the way in which it participates in this direction is not as clear. In the same way, while the terms "strategy" and "strategic planning" are conceptually clear, where the strategic role of the board ends and where the role of executive management begins is not always as clear.[3] Identifying the different roles of the board and executive management in the strategy development process is one of the most important governance issues. For this reason, different approaches are recorded in the literature.

One approach is to separate the design of the strategy from its evaluation.[4] However, experience has shown that the board is not always in a position to fully undertake the design of the strategy and to entrust the implementation and evaluation to the executive administration. The executive management is in a better position when it comes to highlighting the problems and challenges faced by a sport organization.[5] The daily involvement with the operation of the organization provides the salaried administrative staff with significant experience and knowledge on complex issues, which is known in the literature as *"information asymmetry."*[6]

Therefore, if attempts are made to unbundle the responsibilities of the board on the one hand and the executive administration on the other, it is expected that the board's contribution to the strategic planning will be limited. This is because the members of the board are absent from the day-to-day operation and do not have vital information, while at the same time they affirm their need to be an independent board.[7]

A second approach considers that the strategic role of the board remains strong when it participates and contributes to strategic thinking by participating in discussions on the strategic directions of the sport organization.[8] In this case, the strategic planning involves two stages:

1   Informal but targeted discussions of the board's strategic issues.
2   The formal process of preparing the strategic planning, which is less important, while the role of the board is limited to legitimizing the final content.

This approach seems to indicate that the role of the board may become more important in the preparation of the strategic planning; that is, when it focuses on highlighting the strategic issues.

The third approach is documented by research in nonprofit sport organizations and approaches strategy at the board level either as an activity of generating resources of vital importance to the organization or as a representation function.[9] Organizations that operate in an environment with limited resources expect their board to take the lead in seeking and securing resources, while organizations facing a highly complex environment expect their board to be actively involved in the design of their strategy. Of course, the more organizations develop and diversify, the more it seems that its role board is limited to supervision and control.

Finally, a fourth approach[10] separates the strategic planning process from other relevant activities and defines the role and responsibilities of the board and the responsibilities of the executive management. In particular, the board's strategic contribution may take four forms:

- Strategic thinking – analysis of the external environment
- Strategic decisions – strategic axes
- Strategic planning – individual actions and budget
- Implementation of the strategy – implementation, monitoring, revision

It is understood from the above approaches that the board's involvement in strategic planning depends on cooperation and communication between the members, the executive director, and the rest of the staff; it is balanced and diverse; and, above all, includes independent members who can challenge the proposed centralized strategic choices.

It is equally important for the board to have knowledge of the operational environment of the sport organization and the problems it faces. Here, the role of the executive director and the rest of the staff is catalytic because they are the ones who will present to the members of the board the chosen strategy with clear documentation.

The Strategic Planning Process

Strategic planning is already a typical organizational reality in many organizations operating in competitive industries. In sport organizations, however, its implementation has been delayed for various reasons, such as a lack of knowledge and will and reduced pressure for effective administration. Even the terminology of this process, wherever and when it is used, is ambiguous; the executives of a sport organization may talk about objectives and refer to the mission, or even confuse programs with activities.

Although strategic planning and its tools both have a place in the broader organizational theory, in sport governance, strategic thinking is absent both as a process and as a culture. Its steps are not widely known and clear, so our knowledge is derived from the management of the nonprofit sector. A representative[11] strategic planning model includes the following steps:

- Formulation of the mission, vision, and values of the sport organization
- Evaluation of the internal and external environment
- Identifying the strategic issues or strategic questions that should be addressed
- Definition of objectives, strategies, and objectives
- Full design development and communication
- Development of the individual action programs
- Implementation of the design
- Evaluation

The responsibility for drawing up the strategic planning for a period of three or five years is entrusted to the board of sport organizations, mainly in terms of raising the strategic questions and strategic pillars.[12] The board has responsibility for clearly articulating the vision, the central strategic issues, and the expected results for the next three to five years. The full development of planning requires the cooperation of executive staff, as well as of important stakeholder groups. At the same time, only the board can modify the strategic pillars of planning and the criteria for its evaluation.

This implies that the board should define strategic planning as an exclusive topic in its deliberations at least once a year; the implementation of strategic planning should also be overseen at each meeting. It is certainly important to introduce informal or formal consultation processes that promote the active participation of key stakeholder groups and the early identification of issues or problems of strategic importance that affect the sustainability and development of the organization.[13]

Due to their small size, local sport organizations face significant constraints in financial and human resources, both in the preparation of strategic planning and in the formal operational planning. In these cases, the members of the board have two roles: planning and implementation.

Identify strategic issues

The term "strategic issue" is used extensively in the strategy literature. It refers to complex and important questions or challenges related to policies, mission, values, services offered, the needs of the significant beneficiaries, the structure, and the internal procedures, as well as the governance of a sport organization.[14] Strategic issues are required to be up-to-date and arise from a well thought-through study of the external and internal environment. They differ from everyday operational issues in that they require systematic investigation or creation of new knowledge, while operational issues are limited to the exploitation of existing knowledge.

In their simplest form, strategic issues reflect thematic areas where the sport organization needs to act or introduce changes. For example, strategic issues could include the overall restructuring of sport programs so that they are more attractive to stakeholders, or the introduction of programs into a new sport so that the club can further develop and take advantage of the growing demand for this sport. For a larger sporting organization, a strategic issue may be the institutionalization of reforms in terms of transparency and democratic procedures in order to satisfy the chronic demands of its members or important stakeholders.

Sport organizations need to prioritize their strategic issues, and this is where their categorization helps a lot. We could separate the following four types of strategic issues:[15]

- Development issues that are directly related to the vision and mission of the sport organization and entail fundamental changes in the services offered to the beneficiaries, in the profile of the organization or in the sources of resources raised.
- Issues that need systematic supervision, such as economic issues and policies that affect beneficiaries.
- Issues that will concern the organization in the near future, such as institutional changes in the operating framework at national or international level.
- Issues that require immediate action to be taken today and may be linked to access to sport facilities, staff training, etc.

These categories also help us to separate the issues into those that are of high priority and need to be analyzed and addressed immediately, and those that can be integrated into the strategic planning with a horizon of two, three, or four years.

We know that the most important changes taking place in sport organizations do not happen by chance. Organizational culture influences the ability of organizations to identify both the critical issues that determine their function and the issues that will be put to the board and the way they are to be recorded.[16] These factors determine, to a large extent, the strategic choices that will be selected as the most suitable for solving each strategic problem.

Accordingly, it is understood that identifying the strategic issues that a sport board must deal with could be the first and most important step in the strategic planning process. For every strategic issue there is also the possibility of potential conflicts on issues such as: How to deal with a problem and why? What resources will be required? Who will be the beneficiaries? However, all these controversies are positive for sport organizations because they help to ensure that each issue is analyzed in depth and dealt with in effective ways.

There is no doubt that the identification of strategic issues is a complex and arduous process, especially in sport organizations that do not have clear objectives and mission. However, the systematic analysis of the internal and external environment using methods such as SWOT analysis, or the evaluation of resources and capabilities, brings to light the strategic dilemmas of a sporting organization, and in most cases obvious and logical questions are raised, such as: How will we enhance the sustainability of the sport club? How will we upgrade the medical and scientific services of the national team? How will we ensure a quality training environment for our athletes? How are we going to increase the percentage of women in the sport? For all of these questions, there is an urgent need to find specialized strategies, actions, and resources that will bring results and changes to the sport organization.

Conclusion

The investment of time and resources for the strategic planning of sport organizations has an eye to the future and introduces rationality into their management, which requires a genuine and firm commitment from the board. This is what must provide the impetus to start the process so that the organization can start planning its future. Through this process, the board assumes responsibility for planning the steps toward achieving a specific vision for the organization and its members. The benefits of strategic planning are both for the board itself and for the benefiting stakeholders and sport development:

• Where the board operates within a framework governed by informed strategic choices and priorities, it shall exercise better (more consistent) governance. Strategic planning guides the decisions made by the board and produces essential knowledge about the functioning of the sport organization and its difficulties.

- Strategic planning clarifies the organization's mission so that all beneficiary groups are able to contribute to its implementation.
- Strategic planning allows for the regular evaluation of individual actions and programs and their adaptation to achieve their objectives.
- Strategic planning confirms that the sport organization is clearly targeted and is therefore able to account to members and important stakeholder groups.
- Strategic planning elaborates solutions to address external uncertainties and introduces changes.
- Strategic planning builds a framework within which the organization makes decisions on its programs and the allocation of its resources.
- Strategic planning is often a prerequisite for statutory bodies to finance the sport organization.

Successful strategic planning highlights strategic issues, sets goals, and offers consensual and realistic solutions to the required resources. Possible resistance to the process may indicate a lack of training, both at the board level and at the level of executive staff. The board may periodically introduce informal procedures for consultation with staff and key stakeholder groups, where questions are raised and proposals are recorded. At the same time, when the statutory bodies finance sport organizations, they set certain criteria and conditions. Obviously, strategic planning can be one of these criteria for controlling the efficiency of public spending. Engaging in strategic planning and management ensures a sport board is initiating changes in the organization that are necessary, discussed across stakeholders and are proactive rather than reactive to environmental pressures. The process is continuous and only enhanced by increased diversity and communication.

Notes

1 See, for example, Drucker, P. (1990). Managing the Non-Profit Organization. New York, NY: HarperCollins
2 Nadler, D. (2004). What's the board's role in strategy development? Engaging the board in corporate strategy. Strategy & Leadership, 32(5), 25–33.
3 Ferkins, L., Shilbury, D. & McDonald, G. (2005). The role of the board in building strategic capability: Towards an integrated model of sport governance research. Sport Management Review, 8, 195–225.
4 Stiles, P. (2001). The impact of the board on strategy: An empirical examination. Journal of Management Studies, 38, 627–651.
5 Hoye, R. & Cuskelly, G. (2007). Sport Governance. Sydney: Elsevier.

6 See Chapter 3 and, in particular, the *agency theory*.

7 Pugliese, A., Bezemer, P., Zattoni, A., Huse, M., Van Den Bosch, F. A. J. & Volberda, H. W. (2009). Boards of directors' contribution to strategy: A literature review and research agenda. Corporate Governance: An International Review, 17(3), 292–306.

8 Parker, L. D. (2008). Boardroom operational and financial control: An insider view. British Journal of Management, 19, 65–88.

9 Brown, W. & Guo, C. (2010). Exploring the key roles for nonprofit boards. Nonprofit and Voluntary Sector Quarterly, 39(3), 536–546.

10 Nadler, D. (2004). What's the board's role in strategy development? Engaging the board in corporate strategy. Strategy & Leadership, 32(5), 25–33.

11 Worth, M. J., (2012). Nonprofit Management: Principles and Practice (2nd Ed.). London: Sage.

12 Hoye, R. & Cuskelly, G. (2007). Sport Governance. Sydney: Elsevier.

13 ibid.

14 Bryson, J. M. (2004). Strategic planning for public and nonprofit organizations. San Francisco, CA: Wiley.

15 ibid.

16 ibid.

7 Effective Sport Boards
How Can Committees Help?

Introduction

As the previous chapters in this book have shown, an effective board is not just an institutional requirement, but a strategic need. To respond to their role, boards of sport organizations may establish standing and/or ad-hoc committees, to which they delegate and confer powers to manage complex technical issues and to submit proposals to the board for discussion and approval. Committees can make a vital contribution to board function and decision-making, provide perspectives and diversity that may be lacking in the board, and also inject fresh ideas – known as open innovation – from outside the organization. In this chapter, we touch upon three interrelated elements: board-committee interaction, committee structure, and committee effectiveness. Communication within the committee and between the board and committee is essential and guidelines to clarify the rules of communication should be part of any formal written instruction (often called "terms of operation") to the committee's role and work.

What Is a "Committee"?

The term "committee" refers to a group of people who are authorized by the board of the sport organization to address or analyze one or more issues that often concern a specific area (elections, legal issues, financial control, logistics for an event, etc.) or the needs of a particular stakeholder group (athletes, coaches, referees, volunteers). Committees are often divided into permanent (or standing) and non-permanent (or ad-hoc). The former has a long duration of operation and are setup to manage a specific issue (such as financial control), while the latter have a limited duration of operation and are

DOI: 10.4324/9781003254324-7

introduced to support the board on a specialized issue that requires in-depth study by experts (such as the organization of a conference or a sporting event). The committees of sport organizations can also be categorized into those that are authorized by the board to make decisions and have the freedom to link their decisions to resources, and those that merely make recommendations (i.e., advisory proposals to the board).

Generally, however, the aim of each committee is to draw up and submit to the board, proposals or programs that will improve the effectiveness of the sport organization and its ability to respond to the needs of its members. Committees may also provide summary reports of research or knowledge that will help the board make more informed decisions. The terms and conditions for the establishment of each committee reflect its objective, the breadth of its scope of action, as well as the characteristics of its members, while its work is delivered to the board for approval and implementation. The individuals who make up the committees vary, while the title, purpose, and composition of each committee are provided for by the statutes or the internal regulation of each sport organization.

Committee meetings are an important link in the chain of the governance structure of the sport organization because decisions are made that affect the board, and by extension, the sport organization itself. This also makes the committees necessary for the democratic functioning of a sport organization. All too often, however, the members of the committees – and the board itself – express their dissatisfaction with the low efficiency of the committees. This is because their members do not possess the necessary skills or because the goals they are called to serve are unclear. When committees do not function efficiently, they inevitably become a source of dissatisfaction for their members, who operate on a voluntary basis.[1]

Board-Committee Interaction

Sport organizations with effective boards devote considerable time and energy to the establishment and operation of specialized committees because they entrust these committees with important work in tackling contemporary challenges such as how to increase diversity in the sport and on the board or reviewing safeguarding effectiveness in the sport organization. According to William Bryan,[2] a scholar from Harvard Kennedy School, there are five key steps that can be taken to achieve effective board–committee interaction:

1 **The board sets priorities for a year.** In doing this, there are three mini steps to consider:

    a   Priorities informed by the current strategic plan.
    b   All board members have a voice in process.
    c   Priority setting in consultation with the CEO.

2 **Board leaders annually assign tasks to committees:**

    a   Review all recurring board functions (budget, audit, CEO evaluation, etc.) to ensure that each is assigned to a committee.
    b   Determine which board priorities can be handled by standing committees.
    c   Form task forces (or ad-hoc committees) to deal with other issues.

3 **Each committee creates its annual work plan.**

4 **Committees consult board on high-stakes issues.** For example, before developing a proposal: What risks should we be mindful of? What values should guide us? What criteria should guide our consideration of alternatives?

5 **Coordinate/communicate committee work:**

    a   Committees communicate work plans, meeting notes.
    b   Board leaders (or an Executive Committee) identify opportunities for collaboration or coordination.

The Importance of the Committees

Committees are a key mechanism to strengthen the governance of sport organizations because they support the board and the decision-making processes with additional know-how and proposals. Their operation is also important for the overall functioning of the sport organization because:

- They are a useful element of the structure of sport organizations to attract volunteers with valuable skills that will be used for improving the efficiency of the organization.
- They free the board from part of its work to focus on strategic issues and help build good relations with salaried staff.
- They offer opportunities for voluntary participation in the activities of the sport organization to its members, former athletes, coaches, or other stakeholders. They can also be a reservoir to attract new members who will later staff the board.

- They are a magnet for the integration of important individuals of the wider sport community, who may not have enough time to participate in the board.

However, when an organization operates with the help of many committees, which are poorly coordinated and require the employment of several board members, then there may also be disadvantages.[3] For example, it is possible that committees will:

- Weaken the supervisory role of the board regarding the overall functioning and efficiency of the sport organization.
- Reinforce the inertia of the board members and their reluctance to question the decisions of the specialized committee members.
- Significantly increase the workload of the board members when their participation in many meetings is required.

Against the five-step approach mentioned above, as well as the abovementioned advantages and disadvantages of the committees' existence, there is an interesting question that boards should consider regarding their committees: Are committees driving the work of the board, or is the board driving the work of committees? Although concrete answers to these questions would give a good picture about the extent to which the board exercises each of the fiduciary, strategic, and generative modes of governance, there are (at least) three warning signs one should take account for; these are when:

- "The real work of our board is in committees."
- "Board meetings include lots of committee reports."
- "Committee work is more interesting than board work."

In short, committees should not be designed to replace the work and responsibilities of the board, but rather, they should be used to inform and enhance the capacity of the board to do its work.

Composition and Supervision of Committees

The operation of the committees shall be subject to the direct supervision of the board, which shall be responsible for the coordination of the committees, their organization, and the preparation of their proposals. The board is also responsible for setting up or abolishing a committee, in accordance with the provisions of the statute of the sport organization. This means that the board has the power to delegate responsibilities to a committee, since these responsibilities are reflected in a formal decision of the board, in the governance regulations, or even in the terms of operation of the committee, as approved by the board itself and the General Assembly.

The board may enhance the effectiveness of the committees by ensuring an appropriate organizational structure, by regularly monitoring the work produced and, in particular, by clarifying their role in the governance of the sport organization. The board also has the role of supervising the quality of the interaction between the committees – as well as their relationship with the board – and being regularly informed of the issues and content of the discussions taking place in those committees.

The introduction of a new committee in the governance structure of the sport organization requires similar decisions on the part of the board regarding the subject, objectives, duration, size, type, and on whether it has a role to play (i.e., as an advisory committee or one with decision-making powers). The coordination of committees is greatly facilitated when the conditions for the establishment and operation of each committee are clearly communicated in the internal regulations of the sport organization. Therefore, it is very important for the members of the committees and for the salaried staff to be able to read clearly how each committee operates and what are the reasons for its existence and operation, and the internal regulations develop the articles of the statutes of the sport organization in greater detail. These internal regulations shall provide an extensive analysis of all the individual questions that arise in the operation of a committee, such as, what happens when a member resigns? How can a new member be added to the committee? What happens in the event of a tie in a committee vote?

Organization of Committees

Each sport organization can design and organize its committees in order to successfully serve the needs of its members and contribute to the achievement of its objectives. As a general principle, it is proposed that each committee should have a specific structure and should be composed of people with different characteristics, in terms of their skills and abilities, gender, ethnicity, and age. Below are some of the key aspects of organizing a committee in terms of structure, roles and responsibilities, skills and diversity, independence, and conflict of interest.

Committee structure

One of the most important responsibilities of the board is to recommend the structure of each committee necessary for the functioning of the board and the sport organization. At the same time, the number of members of the committee should be limited in order to facilitate the participation of members and communication between them. The decisions to be made regarding the structure of a committee relate to the following questions:

- What is the aim of the committee and why is the committee important to the board?
- Which members does the committee consist of? By what procedure are its members selected and how long is their term of office?
- How often should the committee meet and when will the invitation to the meeting be sent with the items on the agenda?
- How is the quorum (minimum number of people in attendance to make decisions) determined?
- Is it planned to register the members present and to maintain minutes of the meetings?

Roles and skills

Once the structure of the committee has been established, the next step is to clearly list the roles and skills of its members in order to achieve its objectives. The following questions should be answered:

- What are the necessary roles and responsibilities of the members of the committee?
- What are the requirements for members in terms of time commitment?
- What skills, experience, and knowledge are required for the committee to function effectively?

Drawing up a list of the objectives and main responsibilities of each committee can help to identify the necessary skills and, therefore, to select the appropriate members of each committee.

Enhancing diversity in the committee

Committees represent a valuable opportunity for any sport organization in order to expand its ties with the local sport community and to promote its extroversion by creating an attractive profile, addressed to many social groups involved in the sport. For this reason, the invitation of members to staff the committees should be addressed mainly to people outside the close environment of the sport organization, as well as to people who could make different proposals for the problems that the organization faces. Diversity in the different committees requires clear answers to the following questions:

• To what extent do the committee members differ in gender, age, race, social, and economic dimensions?
• To what extent do the characteristics of the committee reflect those of the sport persons whose needs are important for the sport organization?

Attracting members with independent thinking

The independence of the members of the board and committees of nonprofit organizations is a key indicator of good governance and a factor in preventing serious oversights.[4] Therefore, the governance of the committees presupposes the active participation of people who have information and independent thinking in order to be able to take decisions that reflect the interests of the organization. In some countries, such as the United Kingdom, sport organizations cannot be certified for public funds or other support if at least three of the members of their committees do not meet the established independence criteria. But how can the independence of members be certified? The following practices have been adapted[5] to the sporting context and offer an indicative approach to the question of the independence of members:

• A member may be considered independent where the board can confirm, after an audit, that s/he does not have any form of physical transaction with the sport organization.
• A member is *not* independent when someone from his/her family works or has recently worked for the sport organization or when s/he receives certain benefits from the sport organization (such as a sport scholarship or travel expenses for training).
• Previous contractors, suppliers, or auditors are considered non-independent for at least three to five years after the last transaction.

Being "independent" ensures that there is little or no conflict of interest to declare or manage and that the committee can offer objective, impartial ideas, and advice to benefit the sport organization's decision-making process.

Good Practices for the Management of the Committees

Administration of a board is a complex exercise. For the committees to produce meaningful work, careful coordination, and day-to-day supervision are required in order to feed the board with quality proposals and action plans. The committees of sport organizations, more often than the board, have been criticized for a lack of productivity. The following practices can contribute to effective administration of the work that these committees do.

- Check the importance of each committee. Sport organizations often have either several or very few committees; in the first case, some of them may not have met or produced work over a long period of time. Can the powers of an inactive committee be transferred to a board member? It is also advisable for the committees to be small in order to save valuable human resources.
- Each committee must have a clear objective and appropriate leadership. The board should clearly define the mission and objectives of each committee in order to avoid duplication with other committees. It is also necessary to clarify the terms and rules of operation of each committee, to inform its members and to clarify how they are to be implemented. Moreover, relations between the chairperson of the committee and the other members should also be taken into account when setting up a committee. Finally, given that they are volunteers, it is recommended that the committee members should not participate in parallel in other committees, so that they have the time and energy required for the work.
- Effective meetings and constant provision of information. Each committee may meet as regularly as its members deem necessary in order to meet its objectives. For committee meetings to be efficient, good organization and focus on objectives and decisions are required. It is important that committees do not procrastinate with lengthy briefings and with general discussions. The items on the agenda must be well structured and available to members three to four days in advance. Besides, the information of the members can be achieved by exchanging emails in the intervals of the meetings. At the same time, the duration of the meetings must be predetermined. Recording the committee's discussions by compiling the minutes is a necessary process that helps the committee members to communicate with each other better. The timely communication of minutes to all members not only serves to inform the members, but also acts as a tool to motivate the

members to continue being active in the committees. Moreover, the minutes are important for monitoring and evaluating the overall work of the committee. Each member of the committee shall have access to information, either from the board or from the interaction of the members of the committee. Transparency and clear procedures are two valuable tools that contribute to the effectiveness of meetings and committees.

- Periodic evaluation of the committees and reconstruction. Each committee can learn a great deal from the regular evaluation of its work through the use of simple self-evaluation tools. The aim of the evaluation is to identify the strengths and weaknesses concerning the functioning of the committee and its work produced. The evaluation may focus on the objectives, the distribution of responsibilities to members, the participation of members in the work, the reasons for the removal of some members, and the quality of the proposals exported to the board. It is recommended that the committees formulate the value judgments with a positive approach, engage in dialogue with their members, and together look for appropriate ways to solve the problems.

Conclusion

This chapter has introduced the concept of "committees" to enhance sport board function and effectiveness. The question posed concerned how committees can help the sport board and the chapter has provided a balanced view of the impact of committees, recognizing the challenges in coordination and communication within the committee and between the committee and the board. At the same time, it highlighted the considerable value that committees bring to the sport board in increased diversity of perspectives, knowledge or skills lacking in the board that inhibit quality decision-making and the opportunity to build a network of potential future board members. Just like sport boards, committees require clearly communicated "terms of operation" and oversight to be accountable for their responsibilities. The management of committees may seem onerous at first, but the use of committees can be done gradually, while the board learns the challenges and benefits to the sport organizations as well as how to manage committees most effectively. To this end, we have also provided some "best practices" in the management of committees that reveals the importance of evaluation in developing effective committees which is a process, not a static task that once done, cannot be changed or amended. In fact, committees can and should change. New committees can be formed as needed or existing committees can be restructured when performance is weak or new opportunity requires for change to be made. Committees provide essential additional diversity to the board and if communication of the committees' purpose and function as clearly defined (and changed/amended as needed), through formal terms of reference/operation, it is hard to imagine a sport board functioning without the contribution of them.

Notes

1 Cuskelly, G. (1995). The influence of committee functioning on the organizational commitment of volunteer administrators in sport. Journal of Sport Behavior, 18(4), 254–269.
2 Bryan, W. (2021). Mobilizing Your Board (module 3). Personal notes from the Executive Education Program at Harvard Kennedy School. Attended by Christos Anagnostopoulos in May–June, 2021.
3 Wales Board for Voluntary Action (2012). Faith and Hope don't run charities: A practical guide for voluntary members of management committees (3rd Edn.).
4 Peregrine, M. W. & Broccolo, B. M. (2006). Independence and the nonprofit board: A general counsel's guide. Journal of Health Law, 36(4), 497–526.
5 Millstein, I., Gregory, H. & Grapsas, R. (2006). Corporate Governance: Board Priorities in 2006. Weil Gotshal & Manges LLP.

8 CEO and Sport Boards
Who's the Boss?

Introduction

When sport organizations grow rapidly, important questions often arise about the responsibility of governance. Although the board assumes responsibility for governance, research has shown that the role of day-to-day supervision of the sport organization is highly demanding for a voluntary-based board of directors. In this chapter, we focus on the role of the salaried general director (the chief executive officer) and analyze the importance of this complex relationship (with the board) for the effective functioning of the board of directors and, by extension, of the sport organization. The relationship between the board of directors (hereinafter referred to as the board) and the chief executive officer (hereinafter referred to as CEO) has not been studied extensively by researchers and theorists of the management of sport organizations. However, this relationship is important not only for the effective functioning of the board, but also for the leadership of the sport organization.[1] The relationship is neither one-dimensional nor static, but dynamic in that the boundaries of this position are constantly developing and evolving, and this is because both the conditions and activities of a sport organization and the persons involved in the governance structures are also changing.

Therefore, the analysis of this relationship cannot be limited and understood by simply indicating the roles of each party and the work they are called upon to carry out.

The CEO's Role

The CEO holds a salaried position in the nonprofit organizations and works to support the board. The CEO directs and coordinates the day-to-day running of the organization and implements the decisions of

DOI: 10.4324/9781003254324-8

the board. He or she is the senior manager in the team of salaried administrative staff who supports the day-to-day operation of the organization. In some cases, the CEO of large nonprofits may participate in the meetings of the board, with or without voting rights, to facilitate communication and transparency in policy formation and operational issues.

Some sport organizations may employ two executives with specialized administrative responsibilities. For example, a large sport club may employ an administrative director and a technical director. The technical director supervises sport departments and coaches and solves problems arising in competitions or championships, while the administrative director oversees marketing, communication, and financial issues. These two posts overlap with the role and responsibilities of the CEO, which is the case where it is called the "dual executive structure." These two directors can report separately to the board as equal members.

By sticking to amateur governance structures, other smaller sport organizations avoid hierarchies that give an employee the authority to supervise the rest of the salaried staff. In these cases, a small group of volunteers/members of the board – usually consisting of the president, the general secretary, and the treasurer –supervises the operations of the organization on a daily basis.

The role and responsibilities of the CEO should evolve as the organization grows and its operation becomes more complex. The development of more activities, combined with the increase in the number of athletes and the increase in the popularity of a sport, forces organizations to recruit executives with specialized management knowledge in different fields. In these cases, the boards employ more of a strategic mode of governance, with the result that the everyday life of the sport organization passes into the hands of specialized executives, such as the CEO. In such cases, the CEO acquires an enhanced role and is called to account on various fronts, such as the board, member-clubs, salaried administrative and technical staff, the local community, or the professional associations.

The CEO's Responsibilities

Many sport organizations are confused regarding the role of the board versus the role of the CEO, and where these responsibilities may overlap. The responsibilities of the CEO may differ in different sport organizations. In some organizations, the board may delegate to the CEO the responsibility for developing new sources of revenue or agreements with donors. Where the organization employs a large number of administrative and technical staff, the role of the CEO may focus on the supervision of salaried staff and the monitoring of efficiency. Sport organizations should define the roles and responsibilities and evaluate their effectiveness, making appropriate adjustments to better meet organizational needs.

However, based on the relevant literature[2] on responsibilities, some common responsibilities of the CEO are as follows:

- Commitment to the mission. The CEO must have a thorough understanding of the mission of the sport organization, taking into account its decisions and preventing any disorientation from the mission.
- Lead the salaried staff and organizational operations. The CEO is responsible for the selection, training, development, and encouragement of the staff. The CEO also designs the structure of the organization to harmonize with its activities and takes care of the efficiency of its daily operation.
- Exercise responsible financial supervision. Although the board is responsible for ensuring that the financial functions of the organization are transparent and reliable (i.e., the fiduciary mode of governance), it is the CEO who manages the organization's revenues, expenditures, and assets on a daily basis. Therefore, the CEO is responsible for carrying out regular audits to protect the organization from oversights, wastage, and fraud.
- Leads and manages resource development actions. This responsibility may be shared between the CEO and the members of the board. However, in many sport organizations, the CEO may be closely involved in the design and implementation of resource development programs, as well as in the supervision of the team.
- Complies with the legal framework and the highest ethical standards and ensures accountability. The board may design policies that set conditions and procedures for everyone to comply with, but it is the CEO who is obliged to implement them.
- Involves the board in strategic planning and leads the way in the implementation of the plan.

  Strategic planning is an important responsibility that the board can share, to some extent, with the CEO. However, the CEO often coordinates the strategic planning process, provides the necessary information and data, and highlights the strategic issues to be proposed to the board for consultation. The CEO is also supposed

to be responsible for the implementation of the strategic planning and the briefing of the board.
* Prepare for future leadership.

    In some organizations, the CEO has – either formally or informally – some responsibility for preparing leadership at the board level; that is, for attracting new members to renew the board. The CEO also takes care of the replacement of the administrative staff in the event of resignations and is responsible for the smooth succession to the position of CEO when s/he chooses to leave the organization.
* Build relationships with external partners.

    Experience has shown that an effective CEO is one who has a constant eye on the external environment and its challenges. The CEO must be the first to react to new opportunities and safeguard the organization from any type of dangers. Above all, however, it is the CEO who enters into agreements beneficial to the organization.
* Ensure the quality and efficiency of the programs/activities.

    The board has a responsibility to set out the objectives and evaluation criteria for each program of a sport organization. However, it is the CEO who will ensure that the programs are implemented and, above all, that the data are collected to lead to safe conclusions for measuring the effectiveness of these programs. The evaluation process not only serves accountability to the board, but also fuels knowledge about the "becoming" of the sport organization.
* Supports the board.

    Just as the board has an obligation to support the CEO, the CEO has the responsibility to support the work of the board. By "support," we mean that the CEO ensures that the board successfully fulfills its roles (i.e., its fiduciary, strategic, and, hopefully, generative roles).

How "Powerful" Is the CEO?

The position of CEO is the most important salaried administrative position within the sport organization. Although the CEO occupies a central position and gives an account to many stakeholder groups, this position may also be marginalized, because, while it operates next to the board, it does not belong to the board.[3] At the same time, this position is important because it brings the board into contact with the salaried human resources of the sport organization.

Although the board has sole responsibility for planning the organization's policies and strategic planning, it is the CEO who has control over the information that will reach the board. Therefore, the CEO is able to arrange the information to the board and influence its decisions, which increases the CEO's power. Moreover, the CEO, by default, possesses more power vis-à-vis the individual members of the board due to the day-to-day handling with the organization's issues, unless all the members join forces to marginalize the CEO's proposals.[4] Paradoxically, the power of the board is not related to the right to vote therein, but depends directly on the resources, characteristics, and conditions of the sport organization in question. For example, as Brager and colleagues (1987) noted:

• The longer the CEO has held that position in an organization, the more likely it is that s/he will have more power over the board.
• The central role played in communication is an important source of strengthening of the power of the CEO.
• The control of the CEO by the board is often unclear, which further strengthens her/his independence.
• In the long term, the CEO may influence the composition of the board by managing valuable resources and relations.
• The new members of the board are often inducted by the CEO, which also increases the influence of the latter in her/his relationship with the board.

The Effective CEO

Although leadership is vital for the well-being of the sport organization, we do not know much about the characteristics of the effective CEO, particularly in sport organizations. In the following paragraphs, we develop two more conditions that contribute to the CEO being effective in sport organizations: (1) the use of the political framework[5] and (2) the principle of "the right person, in the right place, at the right time."[6]

The use of the political framework

One conclusion drawn from the research on the efficiency of the CEO is the use of the political context. The term "context" refers to the prism through which executives approach and perceive organizational issues. The term "political framework" does not mean petty political approaches, manipulation, or electioneering attitudes. Here it means the need for the CEO to be able to recognize the inevitable interaction of different interest groups and needs in the sport organization. It is natural for every important team within the organization (athletes, coaches, referees, medical staff, fans, etc.) to exert pressure, compete with and participate in negotiations, with the aim of influencing the allocation of the available organizational resources in the organization's favor.

As a leader, the CEO should, first of all, be aware and sensitive to these pressures because they directly affect the organization. S/he also has an obligation to try to keep the channels of communication with the key stakeholders open and to try to influence them for the benefit of the organization's mission. Even if the CEO is intelligent and charismatic, s/he cannot be successful if s/he does not have the support of the people of the sport organization s/he works for.

"The right person, in the right place, at the right time"

The phrase above is a classic administration principle that applies to all nonprofit organizations, including sport. This principle reminds us that the profile of the leader should be in line with the needs of the sport organization. That is, the characteristics of the CEO should match the characteristics of the organization, but also of the stakeholders whose needs and expectations the CEO is trying to meet. For example, a charismatic leader may be suitable as a CEO in a large professional group, but s/he may not be the best to run a local team or a small sport club that is in need of a more participative leader. A leader from the banking industry or even from a charity may face difficulties in running a large sport federation that has developed a distinct internal culture that is alien to the particular leader. Therefore, the CEO is more effective when s/he has the soft and political skills, characteristics, and leadership style that the sport organization needs during that particular period. It should also uphold the values professed by the organization and the stakeholder groups that it is comprised of.[7] This is another feature of governance in sport where sport organizations often value people with "sport knowledge" over other industry or governance knowledge but this is somewhat misleading as there is often a wealth of sport experience and knowledge but a lack of understanding on governance issues.

However, it is important to acknowledge that the above harmonization is a two-way process. Both the leader and the sport organization are changing. Leaders are called upon to adapt to the structure, culture, strategy, and procedures of the organization. On the other hand, the organization will also gradually adapt to the leadership style, based on reforms and changes. The above procedures are necessary and reflect the effectiveness of the CEO, but to the extent that they do not completely remove the tension in the organization.[8] Let us not lose sight of the fact that the full harmonization of the CEO with the culture of the organization may signal stagnation; on the contrary, imperfect harmonization produces creative changes and reforms that coexist with the smooth day-to-day operation of the sport organization.

Effective Relationship between the Board and the CEO

Four factors are important to build a fruitful and effective relationship between the board and the CEO[9]:

- The CEO's perception of the board's degree of involvement with the sport organization.
- Expectations for the CEO.
- Expectations for the board.
- Communication between the board and the CEO.

The board's involvement with the sport organization

Boards should be encouraged to produce work (outputs) for the sport organization. For example, they should be actively involved in activities such as the development of new resources, the establishment of partnerships with important external stakeholders, the creation of a positive image of the organization, and much more. If each member of the board does not have a concrete and significant contribution to the organization, then the process of attracting new members should be called into question and revised.

Motivating board members to bring benefits to the organization may require specific training or targeted guidance activities for members. For example, each board must have a specific manual outlining the responsibilities and obligations of each member, and the annual objectives that each member pursues are also important. It is also important that the members quickly become familiar with the structure and modus operandi of the sport organization and the board. Training and education is not just useful; it is necessary for the development of the board.[10] Members should also participate regularly in board meetings, read the minutes carefully and prepare diligently and thoroughly for their contributions to those meetings.

Expectations for the CEO

In the structure and hierarchy of the sport organization, the CEO is placed immediately after the board. Therefore, the main concern of each CEO is to meet the expectations of a strong and active board. In practice, this translates into a regular, valid, and a reliable report to the board on the activities of the sport organization and on the achievement of the targets set by the board itself. In order for the board to be able to make beneficial decisions, it must be regularly informed on the progress of the organization's activities. The board should also formulate clear organizational objectives to be achieved by the CEO. The board may be placed at the top of the organization chart of the sport organization, but experience has shown that it treats its relationship with the CEO as cooperative.

Expectations for the board

It is inherent in the nature of the nonprofit sport organization to have the board in charge of the important responsibilities of supervision, reliability, and control. This creates expectations that the board be careful when making decisions. In other words, decisions should be made solely on the basis of the mission and interests of the organization and not on the individual interests of the members of the board. Another important expectation of the board is to evaluate the effectiveness of the CEO on the basis of specific criteria, as the evaluation is directly related to the competence of the board to recruit and dismiss the CEO.

In addition to the above expectations of the board, the CEO may have requirements related to the smooth functioning of the organization. For example, the board should set annual efficiency targets, be actively involved in strategic planning, represent the organization in the external environment, and be regularly accountable to important externalities.

Communication between the board and the CEO

Cooperation between the board and the CEO can be most constructive. There is no doubt that regular communication between the two parties can make an important contribution to a successful relationship. The channel of communication between the chairperson and the CEO should be constantly open, while the CEO should devote a significant part of her/his time to informing the members of the board, beyond the formal meetings.

The quality and frequency of communication between the two parties depends largely on the needs of the board. Some boards want to be involved in every decision of the sport organization, while others choose to focus on the important issues and leave the micromanagement to the CEO, which means that the board must clarify which decisions it wants to participate in and which ones will be passed on to the CEO. However, the CEO should ensure that the members of the board understand their responsibilities as a result of their membership to the board.[11]

The Supervision of the CEO

The above discussion may lead to a central governance question: How can the board supervise the work of the CEO? Effective supervision of the CEO presupposes that the board complies with the following five basic rules:[12]

1   Ensures that measurable objectives are clearly formulated, so that the expectations of the CEO are clear and, if done in consultation with the CEO, reasonable expectations are set.
2   Checks that the description of the CEO's responsibilities is up-to-date and meets the needs of the organization.
3   Ensures that the relationship between the president and the CEO of the sport organization is healthy and constructive. This relationship is very important for the sustainability of the organization. Therefore, these two executives should communicate regularly, even daily.
4   Requests and receives regular written reports from the CEO, reflecting the problems faced by the organization, progress toward the objectives, and future plans.
5   Evaluates the CEO at least on an annual basis, with the aim of identifying strengths and weaknesses and formulating suggestions.

Conclusion

The relationship between the board and CEO is crucial for the effectiveness of a sport organization. Even with careful planning and role descriptions, there can be conflict and disagreement between the two parties, which may be healthy for the organization and encourage exploration of different ideas and perspectives. Conflicts should be managed rather than ignored, with continuous and active communication a key priority in the board and wider sport organization.

While the organizational structure may clearly identify the board as central to leadership and decision-making in the organization, communication and consultation with the CEO is invaluable and essential to the board function and to the implementation of realistic targets, activities, and policy that the board may develop. We highlighted some guidelines to define the differences and overlapping responsibilities between the board and CEO, but it is the responsibility of each sport organization to consider what its needs are and to define the roles to suit their internal capacities, bearing in mind that all sport organizations change over time and continuous evaluation is required to ensure the CEO and board relationship is working to its optimal. Leadership roles are one area where increasing diversity should be a priority but is often a challenge. Sport boards should work diligently to identify their conscious and unconscious biases toward diverse groups such as women, disability, race, or members of other minorities. There should be explicit efforts to ensure the structures (e.g., rules, recruitment processes, etc.) do not disadvantage but actually encourage increasing diversity in leadership positions as these positions are then in a place to encourage greater diversity throughout the organization (such committees or volunteers). Besides, as has been identified in other chapters, diversity improves decision-making, challenges existing practices and provides vital new insight to the sport board and organization. Communication can also be enhanced as new, diverse groups require increased level of coordination and exchange of ideas to learn about the organization and to make a contribution to existing activities.

Notes

1 Kakabadse, A. P., Kakabadse, N. K. & Knyght, R. (2010). The chemistry factor in the chairman/CEO relationship. European Management Journal, 28(4), 285–296.
2 Herman, R. A. & Heimovics, D. (2005). Executive leadership. In R. D. Herman & Associates (Eds.). The Jossey-Bass Handbook of Nonprofit Leadership and Management (2nd Ed.) (pp. 153–170). San Francisco, CA: Jossey-Bass.
3 Carver, J. (1997). Boards that Make a Difference. San Francisco, CA: Jossey-Bass.
4 Tsui, M., Cheung F. C. H. & Gellis, D. Z. (2004). In search of an optimal model for board–executive relationships in voluntary human service organizations. International Social Work, 47(2), 169–186.
5 Herman, R. A. & Heimovics, D. (2005).
6 Dym, B. & Hutson, H. C. (2005). Leadership in Nonprofit Organizations. Thousand Oaks, CA: Sage.

7 ibid.

8 ibid.

9 Markey, J. B. & Denison, V. D. (2008). Fostering effective relationships among nonprofit boards and executive directors. Journal for Nonprofit Management, 12(1), 23–31.

10 Koch, F. E. (2003). Building a strong board-executive relationship. Nonprofit World, 21(4), 11–13.

11 Markey & Denison (2008).

12 Koch (2003).

Index

For Product Safety Concerns and Information please contact our EU
representative GPSR@taylorandfrancis.com Taylor & Francis Verlag GmbH,
Kaufingerstraße 24, 80331 München, Germany

Printed and bound by CPI Group (UK) Ltd, Croydon, CR0 4YY
11/04/2025
01844011-0002